Dedication

To the hundreds of students which have agreed to let me teach them. They have taught me more than I could've taught any one of them. I am thrilled to be able to pass along some of that knowledge to you.

Index

Chapter #1: Introduction

"Music is a more potent instrument than any other for education"
-Plato

There is a flow that you can get into that is hard to compare with anything else. It's often very complex, but when you get into it you almost feel like time stops. There is no rush and no effort. It's like your mind gets to step back and see everything working on its own. The things that you have worked on and tried so hard to accomplish just start flowing out of you like it is as natural as breathing. You feel relaxed, and yet excited, as you feel the rush of energy you have tapped into. Those are the moments that people work towards in music.

Chances are you have felt that flow in a variety of things in your life. It may be something simple like a video game, or it could be a specific time on a sports team. I've often found this flow in running cross country. People often call it a second wind, but it is just finding that flow and allowing your mind to take a back seat. Many people think that is the normal state of musicians who are really talented. The truth is that anyone can accomplish that free flowing music playing if they want to. There are some basic things that we need to learn to start. Just like in cross country where you need to learn to breathe right, step right, and get your body in the right condition to run that way; you need to learn the steps in music to make them automatic.

My Story

I had it all figured out. All I needed was to convince my parents to let me take piano lessons. I would learn from the same piano books my older sister had learned from. After that, I would know sheet music enough to play for our church group. By the time I was older, I would be able to play anything that was set in front of me. This seems like a pretty solid plan especially for a ten year old. I couldn't really see any other paths for learning music, and what I was most worried about was whether I was good enough to learn music in the first place. I knew for a "fact" that some people were talented enough to play music, and others weren't talented enough.

Most of what I thought then was not quite correct, and this is what really happened. I did get to take piano lessons and learned from the same books as my older sister. That is about as far as everything went as I planned it. I did about two years of piano lessons, and then I started learning some basic music theory. It was at that time I found I knew a little bit more music theory than my piano teacher did. This sort of scared me because I now doubted how much my music teacher could actually teach me. Most of my classes were just my teacher listening to my music and telling me to keep practicing. I was going to keep practicing whether or not I took lessons.

I decided to stop taking lessons at that time and just learned on my own till I was out of high school. After high school I started music theory classes from Berklee School of Music. You would think that a program about music theory from a top music school would be a well established path and simple to follow. Once again, I was quite mistaken with which direction learning music would go. I finished with a masters in Music Theory, but each of my music professors seemed to have their own version of philosophy, curriculum, and drive behind learning music. It did not feel like a cohesive "course" of study about Music Theory. I learned an amazing amount of information, but it never seemed to fit together very well. It took me many years of seeing all the connections to see the overall picture.

I spent several years managing at a manufacturing plant for high end optics. I know that doesn't sound very much in line with music, but it taught me some very important lessons, and I did need to feed my two young kids at the time. We were getting to another level of certification at the manufacturing company, and the main thing that we needed was better processes laid out and training for those processes.

I spent almost a year creating visual processes for people to follow for each of our procedures. It was interesting to see how you could take extremely complex processes and show anyone with a basic high school intelligence how to do it consistently. The training and experience I was getting from documenting these processes was extremely valuable to my music teaching. It allowed me to easily break down the complex aspects of music theory and be able to teach any music student regardless of age or experience. I was teaching private music students at this time and working towards transitioning to doing music teaching full time.

I made the transition to teaching music full time rather abruptly due to some unpleasant changes at the manufacturing job. In truth, I probably lasted there longer than I should've. Some places seem to literally suck the soul straight out of you. As a rule of thumb, after that job, I decided that if I was feeling anxious or worried about the upcoming week of work while I was on a day off, I knew it was time to find a new job. It was quite a nerve racking change because people really push the belief into you that you can't make a living in music.

I was plunged into the full time work of teaching music students one on one. I would teach anyone from beginner to advanced and three year olds to ninety year olds. It was at this time that I started taking the lessons I learned in music theory and breaking them down to very small sections for anyone to understand. All of those complex lessons I learned in college were a part of every song and every lesson that I taught my students. If people wanted to learn more, we could get more into the nitty gritty details, but mostly people wanted to learn pretty basic things. They wanted to learn a specific song for their spouse, or learn to play their favorite songs for themselves. I started adding in things that helped normal people get the most benefit from music theory, so they could easily learn whatever they wanted. No one continues taking lessons forever and I wanted my students to have the tools to keep playing on their own when that time came.

I found that the first six months of lessons were very similar for most people. It didn't matter if you were young or old there were some things that everyone needed to know. I have to admit that I got a bit bored teaching that over and over again, so I made a video class for all the preliminary things they needed to know. The classes came across very well, and I have had tens of thousands of students work through those classes online since then.

I'm pretty sure my ten year old self would've been super excited to learn what I know now. That version of myself was very worried about being able to learn music at all. I've found that anyone can learn music. There hasn't been a single person who has come to me and wanted to learn an instrument that has been unable to learn. What I also learned was that music is always growing, and no one can learn it all. You can be a master concert pianist but may have never played in a single gig with a jazz band. The depth of music understanding is so large, that it really only lends itself to one thing. You need to figure out what you want out of music and start learning that.

After seeing the reach that my online courses had gotten, I decided to turn my focus on helping more people. That effort has gone into online classes, music theory books, and even beginner group ukulele classes. Even though it has been several decades since my first piano lesson, I can see there will never be an end to what I can learn about music. There is also an ever growing amount of people who can learn and teach this material to others.

"Music can change the world"

-Beethoven

You think you can be a musician?

There is no denying that as humans we are drawn to music. There are almost no people groups, now or in history that we can find, that didn't participate in music of some kind. It is literally a part of who we are. Many people seem to have an opinion that it is only the special or unique people who have the talent to play music, but that simply is not the case. It would be unique if someone didn't like music at all. It is that desire to play music inside you that shows that you have the potential to learn it. Just like everything else, like walking, talking, and doing basic math, we have the ability to learn music. Music can definitely change the world. It will change each individual who learns it into someone who knows themselves better and can express more aspects of who they really are.

Learning music is similar to learning anything else in life. If you can learn to cook, drive, or read and write, then you should see that you can also learn music.

People often have this odd tendency to believe that others can do something and that they cannot. Once again this just isn't the case. If you admire something that someone has done and wish to do it, then there is no reason that you can't start on the path today and learn to do that very thing.

There isn't any way of getting around it; learning music has several steps to it. Those steps can take a long time to complete depending on where you want to go with it. It is like learning a new language. Almost every person on this planet has learned a language, but it often took them several years to communicate accurately with that language.

I find that the majority of teenagers and adults who want to take music lessons have tried at least once before to learn music before they came to me. In the first few months, I spend a large part of that time building up their confidence, so they will believe they can actually learn. This is because we often have more limiting beliefs about music than beneficial beliefs. When learning music and working through those limiting beliefs, people often boost their confidence in many other aspects of their life as well. They often decide to do other things that they had tried in the past and learn them from a new angle.

I don't know where I'm going, let alone where to start

One of the major reasons it is often hard to learn music is that we don't know where to start. If you haven't learned an instrument, there is so much knowledge to sift through that you can easily become bogged down and not make very much visual progress. This is the blessing and curse of today's information. There is definitely more than enough information out there for anyone to become a master musician, but there is almost too much information available which makes it hard to understand where to start. If you just search "how to play music," you will get more videos and articles than you could ever watch, and the kicker is most of them won't be what "You" need right at this moment. There are certain things that you need to learn. If you learn the right things in a certain way, there is absolutely no reason you won't reach your music goals.

After helping people work through their hindering beliefs and self-deprecating thoughts, my main job was to find out who my students really were, what they wanted, and what information would be most relevant to get them based on where they wanted to go. It's a wonderful benefit if you have a good instructor that will be able to do this, and I wish I could be there for each of you to guide you along this path. Not all teachers will go the route of getting to know you and often teach from their own limiting beliefs. The good news is that you can do this yourself, and throughout this book, I will be guiding you so that you can ask the questions and discover those things for yourself.

I am going to help you discover for yourself what you need to learn based on what your goals are, time schedule is, and what you want to get out of music personally. There isn't a final exam in life, and you don't have to prove anything to anyone. Through this book we are going to help you learn and enjoy music as naturally as possible.

Can anyone learn music?

By far the most common questions that I hear from adult students and from the parents of younger students is something to the effect of "Do I have IT?" After a month or so of lessons, people want me to let them know if they have that special spark that musicians need. They want to be validated in their efforts of trying to learn music. When the parents ask the question, it is much more difficult to answer because I don't know what the parents' plans and goals are for their child. I don't know if the parent is asking me if their child is going to be the next superstar, or if they are just asking if their child will benefit and enjoy playing an instrument. My usual answer for that will be based on if I see the child is enjoying the lessons and is putting in some effort to learn more each week. If they are progressing in those ways then the answer is obviously yes. If the child doesn't enjoy it or isn't trying then it doesn't make sense to pursue it right now.

With adult students, it is often much more simple to talk about. As long as it isn't the first lesson, and we have had some time to figure out what their desire is in learning music, the answer is simple. The very fact that they are here taking lessons and desiring to learn proves that they can learn music. I have never once had someone come to me who wanted to learn that could not do it. Now I have had some students with very high goals in music, and a majority of their success won't have to do with their musical ability. I don't know if they will get all the elements together to create the success they desire, but they can definitely become good enough musicians to reach their goals.

I can't say with certainty that there are people who "can't" learn music. You can't exactly prove something doesn't exist. I don't think we will ever find those people, because if those people exist, then they won't have any desire to learn music and we will therefore never find out if they can or can't learn it. If you have that desire then take that as complete assurance that you can learn an instrument. How much you will learn will vary based on many things.

I think it is a common opinion that you should be able to get in shape enough to run a 5k race. There are even programs called "couch to 5k" and stuff like that. Everyone has learned to walk and know that it is just going to take some dedication and willpower to go a little further each day until they can make it the entire 5 kilometers.The belief is already there. Not everyone can win the 5k though. The truth is, most people who have the willpower and dedication to run a 5k, could also go on to run a marathon. The amount of time and dedication they will need will be on another level to reach that.

 Breaking up your learning into separate categories will allow you to learn each part more completely. It will help you see what is lacking or what things you are better at.

5 Steps is all it takes

When most people think about learning an instrument, they have about two steps. The first step is to get an instrument. The second step is to learn to play it. Although there are people out there who have gotten success with this approach, I have found that sometimes a little more guidance is necessary. I've broken down the steps to learn an instrument into five equally important things you need to do to learn any instrument. Those five steps are:

1. Belief
2. Goals
3. Learning
4. Practice
5. Sharing

 Belief is, in some ways, the most important step in learning music. There are so many limiting beliefs about music in our culture today. If you have some of these, it may not be possible for you to learn and enjoy music. We are going to work through some of those limiting beliefs and cultivate affirming ones that will be the basis of your goals and practice.

Goals are the second step, and we have it here on purpose. There are so many things to learn in music. We could literally learn music for years and years and never get closer to what we want to do if we go in a direction we don't care about in music. Figuring out what we want to do in music will make the learning so much more streamlined and keep our doubts at bay while we focus on the things which actually matter to us.

 Learning is where most people spend most of their time. It's easy to spend all our time here because there are limitless things to learn and become distracted with. This can be an honest distraction, but it can also just be an excuse. You are very smart, and many people are the most clever at nothing else than figuring out logical ways to not do what they should do. Endlessly learning things about music that aren't helping you accomplish your goal is often one of those excuses. We will look at the basics that you need to learn and how to navigate from there based on your goals and learning style.

Practice is what first comes to most people's minds when they think of learning an instrument. We will look at how and what to practice to make sure you actually learn your instrument and not just learn about it. Many people think practice will be a

chore, but in reality it can become what we are striving for in music and the most beneficial part of learning an instrument.

 Sharing is the last step. This has two sides to it. The first side is finding the best way you learn and what teaching style works for you. If you find a teacher that shares their knowledge well, then you will progress much faster, even if you find that teacher is yourself. The second part of it is learning music on another level. Being able to share with someone else what you have learned locks that knowledge in our brains more completely than any other way. That may be showing someone one on one what you have learned or performing a piece in front of an audience.

Working through all these steps will save you energy, aggravation, and countless hours of working on things that are inefficient or unnecessary to your life and goals.

It starts with knowing that you can do it. After that, you need to decide where you want to go with it and set up some goals. Based on those goals, you will discover what you need to learn to get there. After that, you just need to practice the things you have learned till they become a part of your life. Then you can share what you have learned. By the end of the book you should be confident in the steps you need to take to learn music in the direction and way you want to.

It is not a new thing to want to learn music. It is as old as history itself. Different cultures approach it differently. There are many cultures where everyone learns music and plays it together. Our modern culture often removes it from our everyday life and separates people who "Can play" and those who "Can't play" it. This trickles down into our thoughts about who can learn music, who can teach music, and who can earn money playing music. These are all things that you can think on at your own level and how it pertains to you personally. A lot of what it takes to learn music is very basic. You don't need to be special or that one in a million to learn it. Follow these steps with faith that you can do it and you will do it.

Learning music isn't all concerts and magical moments. There are many things that just take memorization and hard work. There are a lot of hours spent on specific exercises or songs. What you will find though, is that you can find the joy of music in each of those lessons and in all those exercises. You will never stop learning, and while you are learning, you will be changed from learning music. Everyone will change in a different way. For me, I personally have been changed in many ways through learning music. I've seen a broader world than I ever imagined and different connections with people and things I never saw before. It has broken open the many boxes and categories I have been told were reality. It has taught me a form of patience and persistence that I can carry on into any subject of my life. I know that if I put the same effort and practice that I have put into music, I can learn anything I want to. For many of my students, I have seen a boost in confidence that goes far beyond music and permeates every part of their life, helping them in school, work, and relationships.

"Virtually every writer I know would rather be a musician"
Kurt Vonnegut

This quote from Kurt Vonnegut is very interesting to me. I have seen this same line of thought in many musicians just as I see it in the parents of my students. I have played with some amazing guitarists who often let me know that they have always wished they could play piano, or singers who have always wished to learn the drums. For many of them they actually believe that they can't learn what they want to learn. For many though they know they will have to start at the beginning of that new instrument and don't want to feel like they suck at it, even if it is just for a period of time.

I'm sure that most of the writers Kurt Vonnegut is talking about have put years into their writing craft. It may be that they didn't just become musicians because of the years it would take them to get to the level of musicianship they have already gotten to in writing. After you have reached a level at a skill, it is always hard to start back at the beginning of a different one. We often think that it will take the same amount of time as the first skill did. That isn't usually the case though. Just as I mentioned before, you change when you learn a new skill, and those changes will allow you to learn more skills quicker.

Many people, whether writers, other musicians, or people in unrelated fields don't learn music because they don't think they will be good at it. Many don't think they can learn it at all. Once again this comes down to our most important part of learning music, and that is belief. Learning one thing allows you the potential to learn another 10 things. This exponential growth allows you to learn more than you can imagine is even possible.

Exercises

Even though I love to learn things, I must confess that I didn't enjoy almost any part of school. As I learned things as an adult, I have learned the joy of learning. I have often gotten into an endless cycle of learning material. I would read books about how to do something, watch videos, and listen to podcasts about it. I would be so consumed with how to do this thing, but sometimes I wouldn't even take the first physical step towards it. At a certain point, learning more about something without taking any steps to doing it will just turn into a form of entertainment. There isn't anything wrong with entertainment, but don't get it confused with learning to be a musician. I don't know where you are on your journey in learning music, but there is a good chance you are in some part of the cycle of gathering knowledge about it. There is nothing wrong with this step, but sometimes you end up getting locked in that cycle like I did, and you don't ever get to work on what you want to do, or become what you want to become.

At the end of each chapter we are going to have a section with some exercises. Each and every one of them will help you on your path to learning an instrument, and some of them will be crucial to it. I will include several different types of exercises. Some of them you will have to go out and talk to people, but many are introvert-friendly exercises, and you won't need to tell a soul you are doing it. Many can be done in the car or treadmill as you pause the audiobook and think through the exercises.

For our introduction chapter we have some very simple exercises, but I do ask that you take a couple of minutes and complete them. It will be very beneficial to do these exercises, and you won't get the full potential of the book without doing them.

Exercise #1 Visualization,
(because running around blind rarely ends well.)

Think of three things you enjoy about music and picture yourself participating in it. At first this may seem a bit simple, but just think through different parts of music that you find very enjoyable. It could be seeing a pop star performing in front of thousands of people or just your dad sitting in the backyard fiddling around with his guitar on a quiet evening as the sun goes down. If you have any thoughts of learning an instrument, you most definitely have a few moments in your life where you have enjoyed music. (Pause the audiobook if you are listening to it at this time and take a couple minutes to think about it.)

The next part of it is to picture yourself participating in those memories. Imagine yourself in those memories taking part, whether it's you playing the instrument or singing the song. Don't think about all the steps to get there at this point, just enjoy the feeling of playing the music in your mind.

Exercise #2 Search
(because the info we need rarely looks for us.)

Research what you need to start music. This doesn't have to be extensive. Do some quick searches about what you think you will need to start music. These things may include: the instrument you want to play or access to an instrument, a place to practice, a teacher- if you choose to get one, or the songs you want to learn. As you work through this book, it is very possible that you will change your thoughts on what you need to learn music, but having a baseline of what you find necessary now will get you started in the right direction. Starting that search now will make everything go smoother later on.

STOP

Just hold on a second!

"Did you really just go on without doing that exercise???"

Go back and finish those exercises.

Chapter #2 Beliefs

"I have offended God and Mankind because my work didn't reach the quality it should have."
Leonardo Da Vinci

Do you know what most people believe about learning music when they start lessons?...........Most have almost no solid beliefs, and the few solid beliefs they have are usually negative ones that I am trying to work through with them. The ideas you have about music are going to have more of an effect on how you learn and what you learn than any information people can present to you. We often have half formed beliefs based on the very limited exposure we have had to learning music. Don't form your beliefs based on your past. You can definitely learn music and reach your goals. If you can't form this belief and hold onto it, then no amount of work or teaching will get you where you want to go.

You are free to believe anything you want. It's not a moral issue we are talking about in the matter of belief about right and wrong. When it comes to learning music, I have found that certain beliefs will hold you back, while others will allow you to accomplish anything. When we are talking about beliefs, we don't mean the beliefs you have about the afterlife, aliens, or magic. We are talking about what you think is possible about music and what you believe about yourself. The quote at the beginning, by the great Leonardo Da Vinci, shows what he believed about himself and his work.

I remember when I was about seven or eight, I wanted to learn to play the piano. I didn't believe that it was something that boys could do or should do. I'm sure I had heard it somewhere, and I didn't know any boys or men who played piano. To a seven year old, that was all the evidence I needed to believe it. I brought it up to my mom once, not asking to learn piano, but saying that "it's too bad that I couldn't" because I was a boy. She said she knew a lot of men who could play piano, and she taught me a little piano herself.

Now that might seem a silly thing to believe. I don't know where you are in life. Twenty something years later, I'm glad I had that experience of ignorance and a mother who could let me know the possibilities that I had in music. I'm glad because it gives me a really good reference point of understanding and patience when I hear so many ridiculous reasons people think they can't play music. People tell me things like:

- o I really wanted to play piano, but I know my hands aren't big enough,
- o I know I can't play drums because I don't have any rhythm.
- o I wish I could sing like that, but I'm just tone deaf.
- o I know, I know, I know
- o I can't, I can't, I can't

I hear so many facts that people know about themselves like those above. The truth is, sometimes they want to be told that those beliefs are not actually true. It's so good that I had that false belief when I was young, because every myth about music I've heard since then I have seen evidence to contradict it. I'm sure that right now you have some false beliefs and limitations on yourself too. You probably have some very good reasons to believe them, but that doesn't mean they can't change.

Micah, "you don't understand. I can't play guitar as fast as I want because my hands are too weak." "You don't understand, all the men in my family sound the same, and I just can't sing that high." "I wish I could do that, but I'm just too much of an introvert, and I don't have the personality that can "Make it." Or my favorite one, "That person is so talented. I could never play like they do."

 Believing you can play music the way you want to is the most important step on your path to accomplishing that.

Talent is not as much of a factor as most people think. The good news is that if you have ever tried to learn an instrument before, and didn't get as far as you wanted to, it wasn't because of your talent. It wasn't because of your body. It wasn't because of your age, race, sex, money, or even the instrument you chose. You didn't most likely get as far as you wanted with that instrument because of your limiting belief, knowledge of music, and time spent on it. I would say that in order of importance you should focus on:

- 1st - Belief
- 2nd - Time
- 3rd - Knowledge of Music
- Don't even worry about your talent at all time

"I am not what happened to me, I am
what I choose to become."
Carl Jung

Talent and Skill
(seem the same but are so, so different)

We have all the talent inside us to reach any of our music goals.

Many people get a little confused about talent and skill. When you have both talent and skill it is hard to distinguish them. The only reason we should care about the difference at all is what we can do about them. Talent is the potential ability within you. Skill is the level that you have reached so far in that field.

As an example, I am not the most talented at math in my family. Even though my talent can't necessarily take me as far in math as some of my siblings could go, it doesn't matter. In the end I have similar skills in math to what they have. I just had to work harder at times to get those skills. I have no plans or desires to go into extremely complicated fields of math and can do everything necessary in my life with my current skill.

A simple way of seeing this is that talent is your potential, and we don't know what our true potential is. Skills are how much you have progressed in a given field, and we have a lot of control over that. When we look at some "great artists," what we see is a mix of both talent and skill. There is a very good chance that they are not the most talented at what they do. It doesn't matter whether that is singing, guitar playing, or playing piano. They were born with enough talent which allowed them to continue to get better, but it's the work they put into it that increased their skill.Their talent allowed them to learn things the way they did, and that doesn't mean it is the same path that is best for you.

As an example, you may have two friends who decide to do music together. The music could be a cover band, wedding band, or just playing at open mics together. It doesn't matter what the goal is, as long as both of them have a talent level over what their goal is. There isn't really any way to measure where your talent exactly is, but I have found most people's talent is much higher than they think. The first friend has more talent, and all that really means is that he will learn things faster (provided he actually puts the work into it.) The second friend can also get up to the skill level they need for the band; he just needs to either put more work or more time into it. Once they both are at that skill level, the talent of each musician doesn't really matter that much. They both have the skills to play in the band, and hopefully, they are both enjoying it.

The only reason these two friends would have a problem is if they tried to raise the band's skill level up a lot. Let's say they wanted to make the band pro level and do a tour across the country. It may be possible that the first friend would have the talent to keep working at it and get the skill level to keep up, but our second friend does not. This is actually quite rare, and once again, hard to measure. The second friend may have the talent, but it will just take him too long to raise his skill level up enough. Usually, the skill level of the band goes up a little, and some of the members don't want to put in the time and work to get more skills. They most likely have the talent, but may not have the time to up their skill level. This could be just laziness, but most likely life events like other jobs, kids, school, or relationships.

The main thing I want to point out about skill and talent is quite simple. It's not about trying to know what your top talent is. It's about knowing what your goals are so you can work to get the right skills to meet them. If you know what your goals are, then you can start to work towards them. It may take a little longer or shorter based on your natural talent, but there isn't usually any reason you won't reach them. You just need to be working on the right things.

So don't spend too much time trying to decide if you have the talent for something or not. Decide something you enjoy and start working at it. It may take longer or shorter based on how much work you put in and how much talent you have. Most likely, you have quite enough talent to enjoy it and get to the level you want.

We don't know exactly how high our talent can go. It's hard enough for you to know for yourself but, others definitely don't know your potential, so never let others tell you that you aren't talented enough. It may be true you need to gain some more skill, but that is always doable.

Sticks and Stones

Belief isn't just wishing for something or hoping for something; it has everything to do with your expectation. You have a belief or an expectation:

- For what you can learn
- For how long that will take
- For what it will accomplish in your life
- For how it will feel while you are learning
- For how it will feel when you get there.

There are so many beliefs about the music process, and most of them have ZERO foundation in the reality of your life. If you haven't learned an instrument before, then your belief about all of those things will come to you through other peoples experiences and beliefs. They may or may not learn the same way as you, and they, most often, won't feel the same way you do when learning or performing music. You will often find that their beliefs or "facts" about these things won't be true for you at all. Often the people who tell you all kinds of limiting beliefs don't even play music at the level you want to play. They are just telling you their excuse for failing.

"Believe you can,
and you're halfway there."
Theodore Roosevelt

There are some beliefs that will help you in the learning process and some that won't help you at all. If we can't believe we have the potential, we will easily find "facts" to back up why that is true. We need to believe that we can learn music. Many people go to a private teacher for the main reason of having someone else believe they can do it. That support is enough for them to continue learning and continue believing they can do it. I am going to let you know some beliefs that will help you and that are true of every person who wants to learn music. I have seen these to be true in myself and the hundreds of students I have worked with.

Belief #1

"What you say to yourself is far more important than what anyone else will say to you."

This can be a difficult belief to swallow at first. Most of us have some sort of inner dialogue. What we are saying to ourselves is typically run by our beliefs. This first belief is so important because it allows us to start to change what we say to ourselves and start believing things that will bring us closer to our goals. The reason it is more important to monitor what we say to ourselves than what others say to us is because we need to believe what they say before it will affect us. If we don't accept what others say about us and don't take it to heart, it doesn't have the same effect on us. This is true of good and bad things. If people tell us we can learn that instrument or sing that song, we need to believe it and tell ourselves that before it really affects us. The next time someone tells you something, think about whether you accept that as true for you or not before you act on it. This is true of music but also every aspect of your life as well.

Belief #2

"Anyone who has a desire to learn something can learn it."

This belief goes with every single thing in our life just as much as it goes with music. If you have a desire to learn something, that desire, in and of itself, shows that you can learn it. How far you can go in that subject is constrained by your time, knowledge, and practice. You will find people who could barely walk a mile decide that they want to run a marathon. The belief in that desire is enough for them to start and eventually finish that marathon. No one will promise they will win the marathon, but that most likely wasn't their goal.

Think of the things you enjoy about music. Don't bring any of those false beliefs you have accumulated over the years to this thought. Just think of what you enjoy about music and understand that, since you enjoy that you can learn it if you decide to. It doesn't matter if: "you don't have rhythm," or "you are tone deaf," or any of your other previous beliefs that kept you from reaching your goals. This simple belief is what gets you started learning, and growing in the direction that you want to. Once that happens, there is no knowing where you will end up.

Belief #3

"You aren't at the end when you start. If you start moving in the right direction, you will get where you want to go, and find out that it is just the beginning of your next journey."

It's very hard to see the whole picture when you start a project or new life path. People often have a goal, and when they start out, they get discouraged that they aren't where they want to be. It takes time for everything to manifest. We know how long it takes for vegetables to grow or a fruit to ripen, but we can't measure how long it will take for your goal to come to its fullness. That goal is really just the start of a new life path that you haven't discovered yet.

I watched an interview with Jim Carrey where he was talking about the start of his career as an actor. At one point, before he had any success, he wrote himself a check for ten million dollars for "acting services rendered." In the interview he went on to say that it wasn't just about the money, because if someone had immediately given him that check, it wouldn't have meant anything really. His goal was to be living a life where getting a check of that size was possible. It was the jobs he would be doing at that point; the people he would be meeting and working with.

In that same way, if you had a goal to play in a cover band, about one of your favorite bands, it's not just the act of doing it that you want. The goal entails a lifestyle of playing in a band. It involves having bandmates who enjoy the same music as you and being in a working relationship with them. It involves meeting fans who also enjoy that music. Starting down that path should bring into your life more of those people who have those things in common with you. Starting the band or playing a single gig isn't going to be your real goal. The lifestyle will take time to come about.

Belief #4
No one can judge your work unless you first let them and then believe them.

This can be a very difficult belief to take hold of. Especially in this time of life, we are often seeking validation, and with that comes critique. The truth is that no one actually has the right to judge your work unless you allow them too. Of course, people can say whatever they want, but what you allow yourself to believe is when that critique takes effect, and that is up to you. No one knows exactly what you put into your music except you, (provided you have any awareness of yourself at all.) This is the same for music, as it also is for looks or education. When you are dressing yourself or working out to look a certain way, it is first and foremost for yourself. Look the way you want and don't take to heart what others think because you are the only one who allows those judgements to take effect or not.

This can be more difficult for some people and instruments than others. I have found this is the hardest for people who want to learn to sing. When we learn an instrument, and someone says that we played something wrong or we should change this or that, it is more subjective. There is a separation between our instrument and ourselves. It is also less normal for people to critique your instrument playing unless they feel they have some reason to, like if they play that same instrument. When we are learning to sing, we are learning to use a part of our bodies. We are learning to control a part of ourselves. When people say we did a bad job or we should improve in this or that way, they aren't saying our instrument was sounding off. They are saying a part of who we are was wrong. It is extremely personal and can be hard to shake. On top of that, everyone has a voice, and it seems like everyone feels they have the right to critique your voice since they also talk and know a little bit about it.

You always have to remember that they don't know where you have been. They don't know the work you are putting into your music. They definitely don't know where you will go with it. Believe you can reach your goal and keep working towards it.

Belief #5

"What you desire about music is the first and most important reason for learning music. No other reason comes even close."

As a music teacher I have heard so many reasons for why people decide to learn music. Those reasons range from getting additional study for school to preparing for a talent show. Over the first few months, we work to find the real reason they decided to learn music. Those real reasons usually come down to just a few things: relaxation, social connection, status, intellectual engagement, or enjoyment. Often people had a goal when they started learning music. When that goal is finished, you can remember the real reason you wanted to learn music and keep going as far as you want.

I once had a student who was learning guitar. At the end of the school year he took a break, and when the new school year started his mother wanted to learn piano also. She wanted to learn a specific song, and we were working on that in several ways. She was progressing well, and by the time she finished that song, we found that what she wanted to get out of learning the piano was intellectual stimulation. After her kids had been born, she had stopped working a career and felt like she didn't have any intellectual stimulation, like so many stay at home parents feel. Now that we both knew what she wanted out of lessons, as we chose new songs we could pick them and learn them based on that. It didn't matter if she learned them well enough to play for other people. She learned the songs the way she wanted to and got the benefits from them.

Belief #6

"How long it takes is an illusion. There is no end to exploring music unless you decide to stop."

Unless you have a very specific goal in mind, there isn't a set amount of time that learning music will take. If you can find your reason and enjoyment in learning music in your first lesson, then in some ways you have already arrived. There is no end to what you may learn in music. There is definitely no end to the benefits you will get from playing and experiencing music. There is a learning curve, and at a certain point, you will be able to learn new songs quicker, but that curve is different for each person. It's the act of engaging and learning music that most people find beneficial in their lives.

Learning to enjoy music at each stage of learning will create a more sustainable way to learn music. It will make you reach higher goals just because you enjoy it.

Belief #7

"You are not your family or your failures. You can learn anything you wish to learn."

Sometimes understanding that some of your beliefs may not be true is enough for many people. Just because you have a parent or sibling that isn't good at music doesn't mean you won't be. In the same way, if you had a sibling who was much more talented than you were doesn't mean you can't get just as much out of playing music as anyone else can. Even if you tried music as a kid, or failed at a talent show, it doesn't mean you aren't capable of all you want to do.

You are capable of learning anything you set your mind to. That may be music, or it may be anything else you want in your life. Start learning more about what you want, and each new thing you learn will lead you to that goal.

You aren't your siblings or your family and won't play the same as them.

"I think it is possible for ordinary people to choose to be extraordinary"
Elon Musk

I like a lot of Elon Musk quotes because they are very engineer minded instead of philosophically minded. I'm sure he phrases it this way because he "thinks it is possible" people can be extraordinary, but many will choose not to be. There is no denying that Elon Musk has done extraordinary things in his life. Hearing about some of his life, you will find he is a very unique person, and there aren't many people who could reach his level because many won't have his level of talent or the time to cultivate the skills he has in many aspects. You will also learn that he put more into his passion than most will ever come close to. He mentions that he often works 100 hours or more a week on projects. This, in itself, is huge.

Think about your schedule for something that you like to do, like music. You work a full time job (often not associated with music.) You do an hour or a half hour of lessons with a teacher a week. If you are dedicated, you may do an hour or half hour a day of practice. If you are measuring your progress against a professional, you need to look at the current work you do versus the work they do. You probably are doing 3-7 hours a week while they may be doing 40-100 hours a week of the same thing. It is obvious that they will progress much faster than a person who isn't working those hours.

It is possible for an ordinary person to choose to be extraordinary, but that choice will require changes in your life to achieve that "extra."

Exercise #1

What are some of the beliefs that you have about music?

Don't try to overthink this too much, just start simple. Think of beliefs that are positive and negative.

- Do you believe you can learn to play an instrument or sing?
- Do you think it can be fun to learn?
- Do you think it will be difficult?
- Do you think you need something special inside you to learn music or can anyone do it?
- Is there something you think is going to hold you back when you are learning music?
- Do you have goals you feel are not reachable?

Exercise #2
List what you Believe?

An easy way to see if you have any limiting beliefs is to take a look at your goals. We will be going over our goals in the next chapter, but start now and just list at least three goals you have in music.

After you have some basic goals down, look at them and ask yourself, "Do I have any doubts I can do this?"

We all have a doubter inside our minds. We can use this step to see what thoughts pop in our heads.

As I said earlier, most of those beliefs won't be based on reality. You can learn music, and you can reach your goals. As you work through this book, you will see exactly why.

Exercise #3
Ask a Musician

Talk to a musician about when they started learning music. Ask them some questions about their own lives. We aren't getting advice from them, just finding out the path they took.

Find out:
- Why did they learn music?
- What were their goals?
- What did they believe about their potential?

Exercise #4
What do you want out of Music?

(Audiobook Friendly) Think about why you want to learn music. Are there any reasons you think that you won't be able to accomplish them? After that, think about whether those reasons are real or are they just part of your negative beliefs.

Recap

What you believe will affect what and how much you learn in almost every way. Those beliefs aren't about things that are right or wrong; they are about what you think is real and true, or fake and false. It's important to figure out what your beliefs are when it comes to music so you can form accurate goals and plans to learn it. The beliefs we have are more important than almost anything else. I may break my hand, and it will heal again. If someone gives me an idea that I can't do something, and I believe it, there is almost no way for me to overcome that till I take care of that belief.

There are beliefs that are positive for learning music and some beliefs that will make it difficult to learn music.

Some negative beliefs may be:
- I'm not talented enough.
- Music will be hard for me.
- I don't have good rhythm.
- I can't sing.
- I probably won't be very good.

Some positive beliefs may be:
- I love music.
- I'm excited to learn my instrument.
- I can do this.
- All my favorite artists were once beginners.

- I can learn this.

Learning about what you believe will help you understand what needs to happen for you to be successful in learning an instrument.

Affirmation Statement

 ### Belief:
What you believe will shape how you learn and how far you will go. Believing that you can learn music is more important than your talent, connections, or background.

If you have a desire to learn music, that is proof in itself that you have the ability to learn it.

If you maintain your belief that you can learn music as you work towards your goals, you will continually be making progress towards them.

Chapter #3 Goals

"We cannot solve problems with the same thinking we used when we created them."
Albert Einstein

Many times goals are one of those necessary evils that we feel like we need to do, but we never want to make them. It can feel like an ultimatum when we make a goal. Often, we either make them very specific and any little change in life will determine whether or not we can accomplish them, or we are so vague that we can't help but complete them. Both of these ways can be disappointing at times, and neither one is always the best motivator to learning, which is a major point of setting goals. The goals we want to create will guide us in what we learn and how we learn it.

Goals are something that are essential to make sure you are learning what you want to learn. If you just go to a music teacher and say "I want to learn guitar," you may not get what you want at all. You may want to play lead electric guitar and just learn acoustic chords for a year. It would be like going to a gym and saying you want to learn to exercise and you like the outdoors. They may sign you up for a spin class because bicycles are outdoorsy. After a year of spin, you decided you actually want to exercise by swimming consistently and need lessons in that. The year you spent in spin class isn't exactly going to help you towards swimming better.

As a music teacher, I barely need to advertise during the month of January because so many people come in with a yearly goal of learning an instrument. This is a fairly vague goal, "learn an instrument." Many of these people would work at it for several months and do quite well. The problem came when something in their life changed. It could really be anything from a shift change at work, to a new relationship starting. When that change happened, they would not find the time to keep up lessons and eventually stopped.

Through the years, I started working on goals in a very different way. I started setting goals with my students for emotional reasons. Studies have shown that people who make goals with emotions as their criteria are more likely to continue with their work than those who only have fact based goals. Finishing the act of the goal isn't what you fully want. You want the lifestyle and the feeling of that lifestyle.

The same can be true of diets and losing weight. If you have someone who starts a diet because their goal is to lose ten pounds, it is possible that they will reach that goal. Often after they reach the goal, they will stop the diet and immediately gain the weight again. If the same person decides they want to be happy with their body size and want to have more energy, something quite different happens. They may or may not lose 10 pounds but they will constantly be monitoring how their meals make them feel. This is something that often will last much longer and create a new pattern in their life. This will help them become more healthy and happy with themselves from day to day.

Most people who came to me to learn music one on one (I would bet most of you reading this book also) have tried to learn music in one way or another. I don't know what methods you used or how long or hard you worked, but most likely, it didn't work out the way you wanted if you are reading this book today. You will be happy to know that anything you learned in the past from music will help you now. Don't ever feel like your last attempt at something was a waste of effort, even if you didn't get to exactly where you wanted to go. Every step towards what we want is getting you closer there.

One time, I started working with a new student who wanted to learn a specific song. It was obvious that his main style of playing was ragtime music. This is a very niche style, and he was very good at it. The song he brought me was an advanced piano piece from an Asian/American TV show. It had a loosely classical style but was more on the pop side of music than classical. It was nothing like ragtime music. He was having a hard time because he figured if he just put more work into this song, he would eventually learn it. This wasn't just learning a new song, it was learning a new style.

I could see within a very short time that there were some hand movements in this song he wasn't used to doing. Since it wasn't his usual style, he had never used those hand movements before. Instead of learning the exact notes of the song and learning the "new" style all at once, I just had him start learning the new style by itself with some very simple notes and finger exercises. It actually took me several weeks before I could convince him that this was the quickest and best way to learn the song. In the end he decided to give it a try and started to progress very quickly after that.

We can all be like that at different times. The truth is that you may not have accomplished learning music because you "didn't have time," or "didn't put enough effort into it," but it's also very possible that you weren't learning in the best way and needed to change your thinking and approach to it. A big part of that learning process, that people often need a change in thinking, is in goals.

> *"You can do anything*
> *if you have enthusiasm."*
> *Henry Ford*

Many people make goals because they think that the goals are what they "should" learn. It feels right, like getting a promotion at work is something everything should be working towards. Sometimes those goals we "should" be working towards don't actually get us any closer to what we want though. That job promotion might just be more headaches and more hours. It all depends on what you want and what you are enthusiastic about. If you can go towards what you are enthusiastic about, you will make more progress when things feel less than exciting. If you want to play at an open mic, you don't need to wait till you finish your goal of learning a D scale better. You will learn more things, and learn them quicker if you are working towards the things you enjoy and excite you.

I had a student for several years. He was one of the most enthusiastic students I ever had. Our first few months were a little tricky because it was hard to set goals with him. He was about my age, but was on the spectrum, and it took us a while to decide what his goals should be. One day he let me know that his mother was having a birthday soon, and he wanted me there to help him play a song. I wish I could've, but unfortunately, I already had some previous engagements planned on that day. In the end, I decided to help him play the song, and we would record it.

It took us a while to work it out, but we finished the song in the end, and he was over the moon.

Over the next year and a half, we recorded about a song a week and put them together for Christmas presents for his family. This was such a big accomplishment for him and one of the biggest things he felt he had done in his life.

I look back at this, and it is interesting, because he really accomplished more, in some ways, than any of my other students did. He had a lot going against him, and was, most likely, not as talented as many of my students. In the end, it was his enthusiasm that made it possible to keep working on those recordings every week.

 Working towards something you like and are enthusiastic about often will take you farther than other types of goals. It's the emotions that drive us.

If you haven't learned an instrument yet, this may take more experimentation, but you need to think about what you are enthusiastic about. Incorporating those things into your daily routine and your goals will ensure that you keep learning and keep enjoying your work the whole time. You don't have to worry about whether those things are the "right" things to be practicing or the "right" goals to work towards. If you are enjoying it and consistently doing it, then it will most likely be a large part of what you should be learning in music right now.

A large part of setting yourself up for success is understanding what things to measure along the way. I know that music teachers will often have a specific scale or exercise that the student has to finish before they can move on to the next section or book. If you finish it and move on to the next thing, but don't feel like you learned it well or enjoyed it, you will feel worse and worse about your goals and measurements. Yes, there will be things we need to memorize in music, but finding out what things are meaningful to you specifically will be a large part to your success. Setting up certain things as goals before you move on to other things can hinder your enthusiasm and progress.

I have had students who really wanted to learn certain songs. It wasn't the only reason they wanted to learn the instrument, but it was top of mind whenever I asked what they wanted to work on next. Sometimes those songs were more difficult than their current skill level, and to learn it well, we would need to learn many things first. I would keep working on sections of the song with them, but at the same time, we would work through other songs that were easier. Eventually they would reach a skill level where they could learn the song they wanted, and it would be very exciting. If we had only been working on that song the whole time most people would become discouraged.

This way, they not only learned the song but got to the skill level where they could learn more songs like that.

"A person who never made a mistake
never tried anything new."
Albert Einstein

Practical Goal Setting
(Unlike those fitness goals you set each year)

I have always connected with the saying above. I know it is true of my life, but after studying very successful people, I have found that we have failed more times than most people even attempted things in their life. There is nothing wrong with making mistakes. It's those mistakes we learn from, both what not to do, but also what things we want to work towards.

What you decide is your goal will determine practically everything you will learn and how you learn it. A twelve year old who wants to become a concert pianist isn't going to learn the same thing that his older sibling will learn who just wants to sit on the back porch and play a few songs with grandpa. Neither of these paths are better or worse, but if you taught those same kids the exact same thing, it would most likely be a waste of time for one or both of them.

We will start by deciding a few things which will really help you work on your goals and streamline your learning curve. Think about who you would like to play music for.

- Would you rather play for other people, or will you mostly be learning music to play for yourself?

No matter what your answer was to the last question, think about if you want to play with others or not.

- Do you want to play instruments with other people or mostly just by yourself?

These may seem like little things, but they actually will determine a lot of what type of music you will play and how you will play it. Once again, you don't need to stress over this; just think about what you would like in general.

Some other things you should consider are:
- Do you want to mostly play from sheet music?
- Do you want to mostly play by ear?
- Do you want to mostly play by chord charts?

I always suggest that people learn the basics of sheet music no matter what. It doesn't take that much time and can be really helpful to any musician. Deciding if you are a musician who wants to mostly play off sheet music, play by ear, or play with mostly chords will be a different learning experience from the start.

It doesn't matter what instrument you are using, but let's look at a violinist. If you wanted to learn violin, you would decide if you wanted to only use sheet music or not. Now if you are playing for yourself and want to learn certain songs, it's very likely you will just find sheet music to those melodies. If you were going to play accompaniments with a band or for a friend who is singing at an open mic, you will be learning some very different things. It is not as likely you will just be playing the melody, (what the singer is singing) and it is not likely you will be able to find the perfect sheet music to work with your band every time. This violinist would probably want to learn both some sheet music and how to play chords for the singers. Both paths will be very different from the beginning.

- Where do you want to play your music?

When you picture yourself playing music, where is it? This goes back a little to the beginning, when we asked if you plan to play for yourself or for others. If you just want to enjoy playing your instrument at home or just with family, that will affect what you learn and your goals.

If you think you want to play for others or "perform," you will need to begin thinking of what type of venue you might play in. Learning to be a better singer to perform at a religious setting will be a different study than learning to be awesome at Karaoke night, although both are performances. So think about the setting you may want to perform. Is it more of a coffee shop/open mic vibe, or with a band that plays for a large audience?

- What songs do you want to learn?

This one isn't super complicated. Most people have a good idea of what songs they enjoy. Think about what songs you specifically want to learn. Take a couple minutes to list a few. After you have a few songs written down, think about everything we just talked about. Where are you playing this song? Who are you playing it for? What will it sound like with your instrument?

This visualization step is something that used to surprise me in the past. I would have students learn a pop song with no piano in it originally. When they learned the song, they would sometimes feel disappointed that it didn't "sound right." What they meant was that it didn't sound like the recording which had: drums, electric guitar, synth, bass, acoustic guitar, and no piano in it. Your piano will never sound exactly like that. You need to picture what it will actually sound like in order to know when you finished learning the songs.

Another question you may want to ask yourself is this:

- What is your timeline?

There are two parts to this. 1. How long do you realistically want to learn music? 2. How much each day or week can you put into learning music?

Some people only have a set amount of time to learn an instrument. They may have a wedding to perform at in a year. They may only be in the area for the next six months. Others may plan to learn music for the rest of their lives. Your goal for learning music needs to have this in it as one of the factors. Once again this doesn't need to be a stressful choice; just think about how long term you want to learn this, and start your goals with that in mind.

The second part is sometimes harder to calculate because people are often not the best at daily scheduling. Think about how much time you may have to work on your music each day or week.I would suggest you think about this time as 'active practice.' This is time that you can sit down with your instrument and practice. The reason I mention this specifically is because we can actually do a lot of learning passively or on the go. We will get more into that later, but for now think about how much time you have each week to practice.

Along with your timeline you may ask yourself:

- How long do you have to learn this song?

Do you have a specific date you want this song learned? This could be because it is for a wedding or an open mic night. It also could be just because you don't want to be learning a single song for more than six months. If you are going to be setting some goals and expectations they should be based on how long you have or want to learn the song.

*"Everybody is a genius, but if you judge
a fish by its ability to climb a tree, it will
live its whole life believing it is stupid."*
Albert Einstein

Make a plan
(so something actually changes.)

After you have thought about all the previous stuff, you are ready to put a plan together. Really, the goal is already finished; you just need to consolidate the answers together to see it all in one place.

1. Do you want to play mostly solo sheet music?
2. Do you want to play mostly chords and accompany music for people to sing with (or to sing with personally)
3. Do you want to do both?
4. What is your timeline to practice?
5. Where do you want to play music?
6. What songs do you want to learn?
7. How long do you have to learn this song?

Take those answers and put a picture to it. That could be- I want to play violin solos at events like weddings by myself, or I want to play drums in a Beatles cover band. No matter what it is, picture what it would look like. Then think about what type of person you would be when you accomplish that. It's taking the specific goal of where you want to go and putting yourself into the emotions of who you will be that often helps people continue to practice when life events change on you.

It doesn't matter if you are working on learning music by yourself or with a teacher, there is a learning curve to it. You may find that any number of the things you have decided above may not be accurate for you once you start learning. If you start with answering the questions above, you will be at a good starting point. Once you are going down that path, you may find that you need to change some things. Don't worry about getting it perfect now. The main thing is to be starting and to have a good place to start from. There aren't any mistakes that can't be fixed. This is all just part of the journey.

Exercise Tips

Often when people decide they want to learn something new, they start by thinking about how they will fit it into their life. This may work out, but in reality, there is probably a good reason you didn't learn an instrument already. It's very possible that you need to change a few things in your life. As you look at these next exercises, think about them without necessarily trying to fit them in your current life and schedule. In the end, you may need to adjust some things in your schedule to make it possible to learn music.

Exercise #1

If you had no limits on your time, skill level, or money what would you want to do or accomplish with music?

I know some people don't like hypotheticals, but this is a really great way to develop your overall purpose or goal. A lot of people don't really know why they do things, and getting into this exercise will really help your progression.

After you have a general goal in mind for your music, you can start to break that down more. Every large project will start with very small steps. You can start tracing back those steps from your large goal to make sure the first few steps you take are in the right direction.

As an example: If you decided you would love to play piano solos at wedding or event cocktail hours, then you will start with a few things. You would make sure you start to learn songs with both the melody and arrangement (basic piano solos to start.) Learn a mix of modern music and classic hits throughout the years. You would make sure you have a good grasp of sheet music. These basic things will help you all along but are especially helpful at the start. That timeline may be a few years to reach that larger goal.

Exercise #2

(Audiobook Friendly) What would be satisfying about music if you could only learn it today? One week? One year?

Here we go again with the hypotheticals. There is a balance with everything in life. We work extra now so we can have more benefits in the future. If we work ourselves too hard, we no longer see any benefits. In music, there is a large part at the beginning where you need to learn many things. They are necessary in the long run but may not be enjoyable to learn.

Think of it like someone who wants to make jam from fresh raspberries. If the goal is to make raspberry jam, then spending twenty minutes in the raspberry patch only to eat all the raspberries won't ever get you to your goal. On the other hand, if you spent hours picking raspberries without eating any would be torture. I would balance things out by picking raspberries for a few hours and moderately eating some as you go along. You don't need to stress yourself out just to get a tiny bit more benefit in the end.

You need to be enjoying the process all along. This exercise will help you think about what you will enjoy at the moment while still knowing that you are working towards more goals and fun.

Exercise #3

Talk to someone you know who plays music. Find out how long they played and what goals or reasons they had to start music. What goals do they still have that they want to work towards?

Of course everyone is different, and all our goals are different. This is the real beauty of this exercise. You will often find things you don't expect and also find things that are completely different from what you would do.

You may find that people didn't always finish or complete their goals. This is normal and doesn't usually mean defeat or failure. Many things come up in life, and the path changes from what we first envisioned. Where we end up is all part of our path though, and this is now a part of your path.

Recap

Many people overthink goals. Others often don't take the power to set the goals themselves and think it is the job of their teacher to do it. This is a very important step in taking hold of your own responsibility and ability to do what you want to do.

Most people learn music because, at some point and in some ways, they enjoy it. This emotional desire is very important because people often continue working towards goals that are emotionally based rather than just factually based. The best way to learn music is to enjoy learning music. It is very possible to enjoy each step from day one.

Throughout this journey you will find people that support you and those that don't. There will be people who think your dreams and goals are good and others who think they are bad or unreasonable. These people will be both close friends and people that don't even know you. Nothing that they say or think will affect you unless you believe them and tell it to yourself also.

These goals are going to help you from the very beginning get going in the right direction. You only have a certain amount of hours to learn music, and there are infinite things to learn about music. Your goals will help you start learning the things you will enjoy and need in your musical journey.

Affirmation Statement

Belief:

What you believe will shape how you learn and how far you will go. Believing that you can learn music is more important than your talent, connections, or background.

If you have a desire to learn music, that is proof in itself that you have the ability to learn it.

If you maintain your belief that you can learn music as you work towards your goals, you will continually be making progress towards them.

Goals:

There are infinite things you can learn in music, and your personal goals will allow you to learn what is relevant to you. They will help you make progress towards what is meaningful to you personally. Goals that are based on emotional health and desire will make it more likely that you will continue learning and allow for your music to become a part of your life instead of a chore.

Chapter #4 Ways of Learning

"Education is the kindling of a flame,
not the filling of a vessel."
Socrates

After we have worked on our Belief and Goals, we need to get into the Learning section. Before you jump right into learning a song, there are few ways to break it up. Very often the first thing I do, when I want to learn something new, is to find out what I need to "do." You start gathering a list (in one way or another) of things you need to learn to do this new thing. You will quickly find that there are many ways to learn music, and not everyone teaches in the same way. I have found that many people benefit from different parts of music and very often learn best by different methods. Each method may be perfect for a certain person and learning style. The question is, how do you learn best?

When I first get a new student, there is a period of time that I would often teach some of the basic things to them in about 5 different ways. I will show them a pattern or scale on sheet music. Later I will use that same pattern or scale as a finger exercise. I may find a song or place in a song where we could play that pattern. We may work on a specific rhythm and use this pattern or scale to work on the rhythm.We would often look at that pattern from three or four different ways over a week or two. Sometimes people just didn't quite get it, then one day we would try a different approach, and they would understand. Finding out what finally broke through to them is always a super important part of teaching. After that, we would introduce new patterns, scales, and songs through that method which worked best for them.

Finding out what method you learn best is not only helpful for learning music but everything else in life. This is also one of those interesting topics, where most people will agree, that you should work out what learning style is best for you, but very few people know how they learn best. You will then find out that many people think everyone should only work through their "proven" method. Once again, this is for music in the same way it is with everything else. If you are working with a specific teacher and are having some difficulties, it might just be the method they are using. It might also be your practicing method. The trick is to see what you are learning and see what approach you are using to learn that aspect of music. Often different methods will put priority on certain things over others.

> *"Tell me and I forget. Teach me and I remember. Involve me and I learn."*
> *Benjamin Franklin*

In this chapter we will look at different learning methods, and we will look at how to find out the best way you learn. We will also go over different things you will learn regardless of your learning style. Some of those things that you will need to learn about is:

- Learn your instrument
- Music Theory
- Sheet Music
- Muscle Memory
- Rhythm
- Ear Training
- Creativity

The quote above is not a universal truth but a truth about Benjamin Franklin. This was how he learned best, by getting involved and doing. This is not uncommon with a lot of people, but it isn't the same for everyone. Many people learn differently, and many people don't know the best way that they learn.

Nobody learns in the exact same way. Figure out how you learn best, and you are halfway there.

For the sake of not complicating this, we are going to look at some very simple methods of learning.

Traditional Group Lectures

This is the most common form of teaching. Traditional group lectures are the method schools, colleges, and in reality, this is how the government educates us through the news. There are some who learn well from this method, but the majority of people do not. This method is used because it can easily reach lots of people in a very cheap way ("Then why is college so expensive?"..... "That's a very different topic, but it's not because of the method of teaching.") This is also a great method for giving very basic information to many people. Many companies will have a meeting with all the employees to let them know of a change in policy or something. They do it this way so they can say that everyone knows it, and the responsibility is now on the employees and not them. Unless you are learning music in a school or college it is unlikely you will be using this method.

This style of learning can be very beneficial for learning specific aspects of music. Because of its platform, it is well suited for broad subjects. It can be very good for learning:

- Music Theory
- Music History
- Sheet Music
- Music Philosophy
- Music Basics
- Orchestra work

This method allows a lot of people to hear information and try to memorize it. These subjects above can mostly be learned in your head and are often taught in this way because of that. Depending on the student and how you learn, this may be good for other parts of learning music. It isn't typically thought as the best way to learn:

- Specific Instruments
- Writing Music
- Instrument practice
- Instrument performance

It is not very likely you will be joining a practical course on learning the piano in a group setting like this. You could probably learn a theoretical piano course, but it just isn't set up for this. You may have a course on writing music or songs in this setting, but once again, it would most likely be a theoretical style course.

Beginner Group Instrument Lessons

There are instances where taking a group instrument course can be exactly what people need. This is the method you would begin learning an instrument at school. It combines many things together and gives the students both a technical understanding of what they are learning but also a practical one.

I have used this method of teaching with great success in beginner Sip N Strum courses of ukulele. Some people learn in this way very well because it allows participation from everyone, but there isn't the pressure of being singled out. You get the overall understanding of what you need to learn and how to continue learning music. It only shows the basics to start but creates that foundation to go as far as you want with.

Group Method Band Style

Another group method of learning that is worth mentioning is a band setting. This isn't a formalized teaching setting (yet.) Those who have ever played in a group setting know that there are things you can only learn about music by playing with a group. Sometimes there is a specific person who teaches you, but mostly you are learning by experience. This can be a great method for learning more about:

- Writing Songs
- Rhythm

- Music Theory
- Performance

Since this method is completely subjective to the people you are playing with, the knowledge you will get from other subjects will be based on what they know. You mostly will be learning from experience. It is an experience you can't create on your own. You need the group.

Traditional One-on-One Instruction

This is the normal method when you get a traditional music teacher. Although each teacher will have their own specific way of teaching, it is usually broadly the same. It often works from a specific book and may have lessons or tests to move through the classes and graduate to more books. There are several methods and styles, but they are similar in structure. The teacher tells or shows the student what they should learn. The student can typically respond, and there is an immediate feedback of whether it was correct or not. This is a similar method as the group lecture, but since it is one-on-one it can be personalized to the student with immediate feedback between student and teacher. They can learn much more of what they are looking to learn.

This is based on a very old method of teaching where the roles are set in stone. The teacher knows all the information and is passing it on to the student who doesn't know it. Since music is a very large subject, with varying tastes and sub-genres, these roles are often not so defined. There is always a large give and take from students and teachers. This method is best for older and well established instruments and forms of music.

This method of learning has most of all the benefits of the group learning environment, but also has many more. This type of teaching is great for students who want to have very clear directions for each lesson. Working through a specific book or curriculum is sometimes necessary for many students. Having clear levels to complete can be needed for some students to feel they have progressed.

Some of the things that this teaching style gives you, in addition to the group method, is a way for teacher and student to immediately give feedback and ask questions. It can be difficult for individuals to express questions and get feedback in a group without derailing the lecture or slowing down the progress to the slowest person. This method also allows easy instrument practice and performance in front of the teacher.

Working through specific curriculums has some side effects as well. Some difficulties with this method are:

- Creativity
- Specific songs for the student
- Specific learning styles for the student

If the teacher is working through a book with each of his students, you can sometimes feel like just a "first year." It isn't as personalized to what you want to learn. As we already talked about in the goals chapter, there are infinite things to learn in music, and trying to get the information that is relevant to you can speed things up.

Overall the traditional one-on-one learning style has all the benefits of the group classes. It allows more interaction between the teacher and student than the group class but is similar in other ways.

"Into the Fire" One-on-One

Some people perform better when they are thrown right into the pressure of doing it. That stress can "make" them perform quicker than any other way. Although there are some teachers who prefer to teach this way, I have definitely seen students who just prefer to learn this way. It is very possible Benjamin Franklin was one of those students. They just want to learn by doing. If you give them any new information or instruction, they want to immediately try it out and see how it works or how they do it. With this type of learning, it is very good to have an instructor right there to immediately point out ways to improve the technique or performance.

For students or teachers who use this method of learning, you will find it works best for performance. It is very action based and almost the opposite of the group lectures format. It is great for learning an instrument and getting very hands on. You will find this method of teaching not very fluid. Both the student and the teacher will need to interrupt the other to ask questions or give examples and instructions.

Because this method is so strongly based on performance, it doesn't work well for learning:

- Sheet music
- Music theory
- Music philosophy
- Music History

Just because you are a student who learns this way doesn't mean you need to find a teacher who teaches this style. If you decide to find a teacher, you don't necessarily need them to teach this way. You just need them to be ok with you jumping in and possibly disrupting his flow from time to time. I have found that people who learn this way also benefit a lot by being able to share what they have learned with others. This could be taking on beginner students or it could be just playing what they have learned in front of family and friends.

"Watch and Learn" One-on-One

The exact opposite student of the "into the fire" student is the watch and learn ones. They would much rather see how it is done "exactly" before they give it a try. I have found some of these students often don't even want to try it in front of me on the first week they learn something. They want time to think about it and try it out on their own first before being "tested" on it. It is good to be able to have music that is played the exact same way every time for these students. These students often want to see it done by the teacher before they try it.

In a lot of ways, my daughter learns this way. When she was turning one, she was starting to stand and get around a little more. She would pull herself up on a piece of furniture and try to get her balance. If my wife or I noticed her doing this and said "Good job," or anything at all to her, she would immediately sit down and pretend she wasn't doing anything. She wanted to learn without us watching. She would even do this with learning to talk. She had about five words which meant everything. For a few weeks, we would get to understand what she meant, and then all of a sudden, she would start saying about 20 words. She didn't add them in and experiment with them one at a time. She practiced them on her own and then unveiled them to us all at once.

In the past this has been a very difficult way of learning music. If you needed someone to play a piece for you, then you were very limited to when they were around. Nowadays it is much broader and has multiple options. Working with a teacher, the lessons can often have a nice back and forth look to them. The teacher plays a pattern or song and the student works on imitating it. I have seen some teachers get very frustrated with this because they feel the student should be able to read the sheet music and play from that. Unfortunately not everyone can easily do that.

Now we have so many options to learn this way. If you have a one-on-one music teacher, you can easily just bring in a camera and video tape the lesson. Not only is this a smart thing to do, but you can go back over the video whenever you want to see the instructions again. This is one of the great benefits of the technology we have today for learning. Another way you can watch and learn is by searching for the song on video. It is amazing how many videos there are out there of people playing music. Finding someone who is playing the song you want with the instrument you play isn't typically a difficult task. Finding it being played exactly as you are learning it is not always the case, but it is usually enough for you to get a good idea of the song.

People who really thrive in this learning style will find it difficult to learn songs that are very obscure that they can't find recorded anywhere. One of the most difficult things to learn from this style is creativity and improvisation. It's not exactly improvisation if you showed someone how to do it. Teaching creativity to these students is usually about teaching methods and tools to create and do improvisation. Creativity is a learned skill, and even people with this style of learning can work on it.

"Apprenticeship" One-on-One

Any of these one on one ways of learning could be slightly different if viewed more as an apprenticeship. This changes the dynamic of teaching slightly. In an apprenticeship, you have someone who has gone through the learning cycle and is just imparting that information to you. All the relevant information is there, but the teacher is showing the apprentice specific tips and tricks to get a polished performance. Many music teachers teach this way. They are just showing you what they have learned and passing it on to you the best way they can. They loved music and learned a lot through the years, and now they are teaching you.

One of the most unique things about learning in an apprenticeship style is that you need to be working with the right teacher. You aren't just learning from them, but you are, in some ways, learning to become them. It's about stepping into their shoes and learning from their life. If you were a music student and wanted to have your own band, but had the opportunity to apprentice with an orchestra director for a local theater, you would need to understand what that meant. It is a very different job than what your goal is, but it may teach you some valuable skills. From that type of learning you would learn technical music skills along with organizational skills. Trying to learn how to be a rock star from your orchestra director won't be very helpful because they haven't done that themselves. You can still learn from them, but you wouldn't be learning as an apprentice because you don't plan to become what they are. You will just be learning helpful skills about music and production.

Learning in the form of apprenticeship will get you exclusive knowledge that only that person can give you. Also, you will typically only get knowledge that they have, and therefore, may miss out on some other pertinent things if you don't align up with their path exactly. They can often only give you knowledge and experience from the things they have learned.

Do-It-Yourself learning

We have never lived in a more abundant place in life than now for learning on your own. You have so many books, videos, and examples to see and hear. It is often very easy to find all these things for free. Just because you are learning on your own doesn't mean you know the best method or path for yourself. Learning on your own just means you need to get the material to learn, learn it the best way for yourself, and then be the critique and decide if you actually are learning it correctly. In many ways it can be the most difficult way to learn, but can also be one of the best. It is just based on your situation and your personality. Of course, learning on your own is great for any student learning supplemental material. Learning how to learn and gather information is one of the most valuable things you can do for yourself.

Although I believe this book will help all musicians who decide to work through it, most likely it will help the do-it-yourself musician most. It is often hard to learn on your own because you don't know what you don't know. There is so much information out there that it can be very difficult to know what to search for. By the time you are done working through this book you will know enough about how music teaching works and what you want to learn for yourself that you can find out everything you need. It is all out there, and you can definitely become the musician you want to become by finding that knowledge and learning it.

"Any Fool can Know, the Point is to Understand" Albert Einstein

If you are just starting to learn music, you may find things to be a bit overwhelming at times. If you start talking to musicians, you will quickly find those who "know" a lot often don't seem to really "get" music. You will also find people who are good at music sometimes don't seem to "know" much about it. Part of this is because of our slightly broken music educational system and our lack of a good broad view of music and musicians. Learning what to learn and why will help you understand at least yourself and your music. It will also help you be able to find people and resources that can teach you those things.

We can break down what we are learning into three main categories: Memorization, Muscle Memory, and Creativity.

Memorization categories include Your Instrument, Music Theory, and Sheet Music. These often can be learned anywhere and don't require you to sit in front of your instrument to work on them.

Muscle Memory is something you need to work on with any instrument because your body needs repetition to really remember some things. Along with this is working on rhythm. You can learn the fundamentals of rhythm on paper, but you really should get your body involved to understand it.

Creativity is something that many people are confused about. Even if they play an instrument well, people will often think that they can't create on their own. Creativity is like anything else, and you can work on different parts to strengthen your skill of creativity. This also involves ear training and improvisation, as these are just skills that you can learn.

All of these things, along with actual songs, are what we will be putting into our practices every time. We can combine them together to allow our practice times to be fun and productive.

But what do I actually learn?

How Your Instrument is Set Up

When you are deciding you want to learn an instrument, the first place to start is understanding the actual instrument. Most instruments are set up very simply. You can look up the basics of any instrument and find out what you need to start.

- You can start by finding an image of your instrument with all the parts labeled. Depending on your type of instrument, this will be more important, or not, but the important thing is to know what the different parts of your instrument do.

- Learn the notes of music on your instrument. Understanding how to play notes on your instrument is very important, and you can find very simple diagrams showing how this works. The image below shows all the natural notes on the guitar for the first 12 frets.

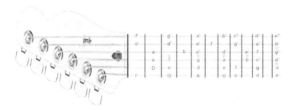

- Lastly, you should learn how to tune your instrument (if your instrument isn't digital.) Almost every acoustic instrument will need to be tuned from time to time (even drums.) Typically this isn't difficult, and the average musician can do it themselves.

Music Theory

This is probably the most misunderstood section of music by musicians and non musicians alike. Most places where it is taught, it is quite separate from the rest of music. Some people even teach music theory as being the same as sheet music. Music theory and sheet music are not the same at all. Sheet music is the written form of communicating music. Music theory is the understanding of how music fits together and how it works. Music Theory should be incorporated into most parts of learning music and not just sheet music. This is one of the simplest things you can do to kickstart your music. It allows you to see what is coming in the music before you get to it and be ahead of the game.

The basics of music theory you should learn come down to a few things. Most songs you will learn will be in a single **key or scale**. That means most songs are only using seven unique **notes** (usually.) Learning all the notes in that **scale** will now let you know all the notes you will be playing in the song. Those seven notes will make up most of your **melody and harmony**. The notes that accompany the melody is the harmony, and they are typically grouped together in **chords**. For each scale you have just a few variations of seven chords. Of these seven chords, usually four or five will be consistently used in your song. Once you understand how the chords work with the scales, you will now know most of the harmonies that will be played in the song.

This can be quite an extensive part of music, but learning the basics is simple enough. There is not enough space in this book to put in everything you need to know about music theory and explain it thoroughly. You can learn everything you need from my website www.speakingmusic.online. It's available in both video and book format.

If you haven't heard some of the terms like scales and chords before, it may sound like a lot, but if you can just get a good grasp of chords and scales, everything in music will be so much easier to understand. Depending on your style of learning, this can be something you can learn on your lunch breaks, or you can incorporate it into your practice and even your songs.

Every music teacher will teach you some music theory. Where many musicians and music teachers fall short is really getting an overall understanding of it and showing how to use it in your daily music. Learning a scale is simple enough but it only becomes useful when you see how it fits in the song you are playing and how the chords work off of it.

Music theory will kickstart your learning curve more than any other practice.

Sheet Music

Sheet music is not complicated, it is just the written representation of music. If music was a language, then sheet music would just be learning to read and write. Just like writing a new language, it can take a little while to get fluent at reading it. In the same way that reading a recipe helps you cook a meal, reading sheet music just gives you instructions on how to play a specific piece of music.

Learning how to read sheet music will be much more important for some people and instruments than other ones. A pianist will benefit from learning sheet music more than a drummer. A classical guitarist will use sheet music 100x more than a punk rhythm guitarist. The same would go with classical pianists over rock keyboardists. With that being said, the basics of learning sheet music are very easy and beneficial for any musician. This would be the equivalent of learning the alphabet in a new language. You could learn to speak a new language, but if you want to communicate with the average person you will need to learn to read it too.

Learning sheet music doesn't need to be much. It can be as simple as:

- The setup of Sheet Music
- Time Signature
- Note Names
- Timing
- How those notes transfer to your instrument

If you can just learn these things, you will be able to communicate with other musicians and learn new songs much easier. There is, once again, not enough space in this book to go over in detail how to learn sheet music, but you can find all that on my website.
www.speakingmusic.online

Muscle Memory

This part of learning an instrument is where time with your instrument becomes quite important. There are parts of being a musician you can't learn in a book because your muscles need to learn it. People often use the expression "It's just like riding a bicycle." What they are saying is once you have learned to ride a bike your muscles won't ever forget, and you can just hop on and ride it again. When we first learn to ride a bike, it can take a while. This is also the same with any instrument.

Luckily, we can start learning muscle memory before anything else. We don't have to learn sheet music and understand exactly how every part of our instrument works to start learning muscle memory. There are different exercises and patterns you can do on day one to start building that muscle memory. This is even true for singers (possibly more important for them.) The muscles you use to control your voice need repetition to do what you want them to every time.

Rhythm

There are a few different aspects of rhythm. One thing to first understand is that you can learn rhythm. Many people think it is something you are born with or without. It is true that some people find it easier to pick it up, but we all have it inside, and it will mostly be about finding the best way for your body to understand it.

Another aspect of rhythm is learning to play in a simple and consistent way. With any instrument you need to be able to make consistent beats. You don't need to know what songs you will play yet before you can start working on these rhythms. It's just a matter of learning how to play the same rhythm over and over again in a consistent way. Some rhythms in songs are simple enough to play, but trying to play the same way for an entire song can be difficult at first. This is easy to incorporate into your muscle memory exercises. Once you are comfortable with an exercise, you can start working on it with a consistent rhythm. Sometimes working with a drum beat or metronome is helpful with this.

Metronomes can be very helpful but are also very boring. Try searching for a "drum loop" on youtube in a style you enjoy and it will be much easier to practice with it.

Ear Training

One aspect of lessons that are often left out of music books is ear training. One reason this is left out often is because it is difficult to put into a lesson plan that is based in a book. Many people think that having a good ear is this special thing, but once again, it is a skill that can be learned. Ear training is simply learning to hear how music works together and start to recognize specific things in your songs.

When you start getting better, it will be helpful for so many things:

- Tuning your instrument
- Note recognition
- Playing "by ear"
- Playing in a group
- Writing songs

Starting to work on this is very simple. You can start with just listening as you tune your instrument. (provided your instrument is one that you tune.) Most people use digital tuners to make sure their instrument is perfectly in tune. I agree that these are some of the easiest to use and great for if you are playing with other instruments. If you want to start practicing ear training, you can just start tuning and listen to it as you adjust each note. You can start tuning your instrument and using your electric tuner to check your work instead of having it do it all for you.

Another simple way of working on ear training is by copying notes. You can listen to a note or two from a song and try to find them on your instrument. This can take a little while at first, but as you work at it, you will start hearing more and more. It is really an exercise in listening. You start to hear how things sound and work together. You will find it isn't that you couldn't hear it before, it is just that you weren't listening. When I do this, I often hear the notes from the song and copy them with my voice. After I do that, I match it to my instrument. For some reason this works much better for me.

Creativity

This is another aspect of music that is not often taught. Like everything else, it is something that you can learn as a skill. Many people don't believe they are good at creativity. The truth is that most people have never tried to be creative, and like all skills, it needs to be worked on to grow.

When you want to work at creativity, you can start with the smallest of things. You can start creating with something as simple as rhythm. When you are working on your muscle memory, you can start creating a different rhythm and do your exercise with that new rhythm. Once you start creating with small things, like rhythms, you can start working on notes and melodies. It just starts with working on growing your skill and progressing from there.

Many people feel they don't need to learn creativity. The truth is that now, more than ever, it is necessary to put your own creativity into your music. Right now we can have a professional recording of any song we want played at any time. We can't always compete with the best recordings in the world, but nothing can compete with the creativity inside of you. Learning some creativity is just learning how to express yourself. When we learn a little creativity, we can put some of ourselves into the music we play.

Creativity creates more creativity. If you haven't ever done it before, it can take a little while to get it started.

Exercise #1
What ways do you learn?

This is another exercise you can do right in your head, so if you are in the subway car or on break at work it won't be embarrassing. Think back on different things you have learned in your life and figure out which ways you learn best. This doesn't have to be just music of course. It can be your first job at a fast food restaurant or learning to drive a vehicle. We tend to learn best in a specific way in most things we do.

I know for me there is a combination of having the material written down and seeing someone do it without the pressure of me needing to do it right away. If it is something I want to learn, I usually do some prep work and get the written instructions of how to do it. After that I like to see someone doing it. This could be in person or just a video online. After I've seen it done a few times, I go try it out myself.

Think about which ways you have learned best based on different skills you've worked on in the past.

- Group lectures
- Group Band setting
- Traditional One-on-One
- Into the Fire
- Watch and Learn
- Apprenticeship

Exercise #2
What can you search for?

After you have decided which ways you learn best, you can start researching them. If you decide you learn best with one-on-one apprenticeship lessons you can start searching for someone in your area that teaches your instrument. This will probably take more than just a google search. You will have to call up some local teachers and let them know what you are looking for.

In the same way, if you decide that watching and learning is the best way that you learn, you can start looking that up. You can search for videos on how your instrument is set up, and how to play your favorite song step by step.

These initial searches are going to be barely a drop in the bucket compared to what you will eventually learn, but it will be that first step. Learning more about what's out there will teach you about things you don't even know you should search for yet.

Exercise #3
What do you need to gather?

Similar to exercise #2, we are going to start gathering things for your instrument.

You can start with finding a good way to learn the parts of your instrument and how to tune it. This can be picture form, book form, video form, or someone to teach you.

Next, look for information on sheet music. Ideally you can find a chart or video to see how the notes on your instrument line up with the notes on sheet music.

Lastly, look up some music theory information. If you can look up some chords or scales that are shown from your instrument, you may get more benefit from that. Look it up in a few ways so you can better see which way is best for you to learn from.

Recap

When learning an instrument, we want to start out with figuring out how we learn best. Take that style of learning and work on your instrument in that method. Once you start learning the material for your instrument you will want to break it up into different categories so you learn each one efficiently. I break up those categories into:

- Music theory for knowledge
- Sheet Music for communication
- Muscle Memory for consistency
- Rhythm for function
- Ear Training for Optionality
- Creativity for self-expression

I started playing very simple songs when I started learning piano. I used to play specific parts of some songs over and over. Those parts had beautiful flow and were super relaxing to me. When I first learned the song, my family was proud of me, but by the 50th time I played that part, they were less amazed. I realized later on that I really did like a specific style of music to play and that I mostly like playing for myself. When I start to learn a new song, I will typically enjoy learning it and not just knowing how to play it. If I can't enjoy the process of learning a song, I tend to not learn the song.

When I started teaching, I found many of my students had very different views of what learning should look like. Some were just starting to discover music. They came to class excited to show what they had worked on and eager to learn a new trick or method in music. Others viewed the learning process as something you must endure, which was the real price of "Knowing How to Play Music." Of those two mindsets, it was always the same results. The ones who viewed practice as a chore would drop out or stop after they finished their first main goal. The ones who came to class because they wanted to learn music, the ones who loved it, would continue to smash their goals and make new ones they never originally dreamed of making.

It was obvious, after a while, that my main purpose as a teacher was not to just give people the info they needed. People could easily find books and videos to find that info. I found that the real job was to make every lesson a time that my students could find what they wanted out of music right where they were that day. It was understanding what they could get out of music right then and sculpt it to their long term goals.

If you can figure out what way you learn best, you will save yourself countless hours and dollars. This will be true for both music and for anything else you want to learn in life. Work with your strengths and you will find you will progress much better. So now let's add to our affirmation statement below about learning.

Affirmation Statement

Belief:

What you believe will shape how you learn and how far you will go. Believing that you can learn music is more important than your talent, connections, or background.

If you have a desire to learn music, that is proof in itself that you have the ability to learn it.

If you maintain your belief that you can learn music as you work towards your goals, you will continually be making progress towards them.

Goals:

There are infinite things you can learn in music, and your personal goals will allow you to learn what is relevant to you. They will help you make progress towards what is meaningful to you personally. Goals that are based on emotional health and desire will make it more likely that you will continue learning and allow for your music to become a part of your life instead of a chore.

Learn:

The majority of material that you learn will be based on the goals you have set and will continually bring you closer to those goals.

Breaking up what you learn into separate sections will make you learn each quality better.

Music theory for knowledge
Sheet Music for communication
Muscle Memory for consistency
Rhythm for function
Ear Training for Optionality
And Creativity for self-expression

The style and method that you learn your instrument with should be based on how you personally learn best. Many of the things you will learn don't need to be learned while touching your instrument and can be taken with you anywhere.

Each new thing you learn allows you the opportunity to learn countless more things.

We have learned so many things in our lives already, and music is no different. Take that as assurance that you can learn what you want to in music, just as you have learned so many things in the past.

Chapter #5 Memorize

*"Anyone who keeps learning
stays young"*
Henry Ford

When you start learning music there are some things you just need to memorize. There isn't really any way around it. Some of those things are relatively simple, like the notes on your instrument, or the pattern of a chord on your guitar. Other things can be more complex for some people, like learning a scale or the key to a song.

There are many benefits of learning new things and memorizing them. Just like Henry Ford said above, learning will keep you young. People often view learning music as something the children do. Of course, anyone can learn music though, I have taught many adults and many seniors to learn music. My grandmother started to get Alzheimer's when I was about three years old. She was confused about many things and forgot a lot, but one thing that never left her was music. If she heard the smallest part of a song she knew, she could whistle the rest of it, and would often be whistling it for the rest of the day. Sometimes the quick and easy route looks good, but there is actually nothing wrong with learning. Each new thing we learn allows us the potential to learn more things.

One of the benefits of the parts of music you have to memorize is the fact that you can do it anywhere you like. You don't have to wait for a scheduled practice time with your instrument. You can do it anywhere and at almost any time. I've often brought music to work with me and worked on it while I was at lunch. Some of my students have said they worked on different parts of music while they were waiting for class to start or on the car ride to school. Once you start working on it, you will find you have a lot of time to memorize and learn these things.

Another great benefit to memorizing parts of music is the ability to not need to think about it. We all have certain things we have memorized and punch in without needing to think about: passwords to our phone or computer, the route to work or school, or even how to make our favorite meal. When you have something memorized completely in music, you can focus on other things. I don't know about you, but I can only focus on a few things at a time. If I'm trying to remember how many sharps or flats are in a song, I won't be able to put as much effort into how the song should feel or be played. The more foundational things you learn the more freedom you have to play the way you want to. Getting certain things memorized will allow us to get into that flow of playing we all want to get into.

This is another part of music that you don't need to be "musical" to accomplish. This can actually be a good or a bad thing for some people. People who are great at memorizing, but possibly don't have the easiest time with rhythm, may get a little frustrated when they try to apply what they have memorized. They feel that, since they memorized the information so fast, they should be able to play it just as easily. On the flip side, the people who are naturally very talented in music, but have a hard time memorizing things, may try to skip over much of this part. Regardless of your specific strengths or weaknesses, the important thing to understand is that memorizing things isn't tied to how good a musician you can be; it is just a tool that will help you along the way.

I remember when I was in my early twenties, I was doing music classes in college, working full time, and we had an infant and a toddler at the house. I was working a night shift that would start at 4:00 pm and I would get off work at 2:00 am. It was over a half hour drive home, and on several occasions, I remember turning off the highway onto my exit and thinking, "Wow, I'm already at my exit. I don't even remember getting on the interstate." Realistically I was overworking myself, and probably shouldn't have been driving at all, but it goes to show that once you've memorized something so fully, like your route to work or home, you barely need to think about it anymore. That is the level of memorization we all hope for in music.

I'm sure anyone would want to know music so well that they didn't need to think about it at all and could just play for the fun of it. At certain levels that will be true of you in the future, but there is so much to learn about music that it will only be the things that you focus on and work on specifically. The next chapter about muscle memory will help a lot with that, so if you feel there is too much to memorize, don't worry about it. You can let your muscles do the heavy lifting, not just your brain.

"Learn continually, there is always one more thing to learn!"
Steve Jobs

Truthfully, I think this statement by Steve Jobs could be both inspiring or depressing depending on how you are feeling. I understand that at some points it will feel like there is too much to learn and you will never get anywhere. There really is always going to be one more thing you can learn in music, and that is one of the wonderful things about it. The good thing is that you can start with learning the smallest thing about music and get going from there. Don't ever feel like you need to learn a certain amount of things before you start playing music.

Learning isn't something that we do and get done with. Learning is a discovery, and there are always more things to discover in music.

Learning music is very comparable to learning a new language. You are now communicating through music instead of with just your spoken language. Your brain is literally going to need to make new connections. Certain words are going to have new meanings to you. When you hear specific sounds, you will be able to link them to certain words or places on your instrument. This is one of the reasons that learning a second instrument is so much easier. It is because you have already made a lot of those pathways in your brain necessary to learn it. Just like with learning a new language, you have a mountain to climb and need to decide where to start and which peak you want to go to first. Make sure you enjoy the view while you are climbing.

When I was little and my mother taught me to play a couple of simple songs on the piano, I first memorized how to find my place on the piano. Now our piano wasn't new, and there were a few keys that were missing their white tops to them. I used those to help me decide where I was on the keyboard. I placed my hands according to how close they were to the broken keys. When I went to play those simple songs on a new piano it was quite difficult to find my place. I had memorized how to play the songs but not correctly what the keys were on the piano. Eventually I needed to learn the notes correctly on the piano and no harm was done but it made for some awkward situations when I was asked to play a song for friends or family.

Memorize your Instrument

So the question comes down to both where should you start and what should you memorize?

I think that for anyone wanting to learn a specific instrument, and I am assuming that most people who picked up this book are planning to learn an instrument, will need to first memorize their instrument. Now there are going to be several different things that you will be memorizing at the beginning, and you can start learning the basics from each category, but we are going to start by learning our instrument.

Depending on your instrument, there will be more or less to learn, of course but a good place to start is by learning the names of each of the instrument parts. On a piano there are pretty much just white notes, black notes, and three pedals underneath. On a guitar though we have: a bridge, sound hole, strings, frets, tuners, and the neck. Since you have come this far already, I have full faith that you can find the resources and get the answers to the parts of your instrument either from another person or from the internet. The biggest reason to have these names down is so, when you are looking for instruction later on, you understand what people are referencing when they say to push, hit, twist, or play a part of your instrument.

The next thing to memorize about your instrument is the notes on your instrument. This will vary wildly based on your instrument. A trumpet can make different sounds based on your mouth position, and a violin will sound different if you move your finger at all. The important thing to understand, at this point, is how to at least find your notes when you need to. A piano is fairly simple, in the fact that there is only one way to hit any given note. With a guitar, you could play the exact same note in two or even three different places on the neck. If you are learning an instrument that plays chords, you can start memorizing chords at this time also.

This may seem a little vague, but because of the vast difference of instruments, it wouldn't be practical or interesting to put a comprehensive list or every instrument in here.

We will look later on about different ways to memorize, but you are going to have to learn the best way to memorize for yourself. If it takes you a long time to memorize some parts of your instrument, it will make learning music take longer. There isn't any way to skirt around that. You will learn it one way or another, and finding the best way for you is going to be your best asset.

Memorize Key Parts of Music Theory

There is a lot that goes into music theory. It is the understanding of how everything in music works together. If you can get a good grasp on music theory, everything else in music will come easier and quicker to you. Because I, once again, don't want to clog up this chapter with excessive details, I am just going to run over what are the key things to look up and memorize based on your instrument. There is a rundown of key points of music theory in the back of the book.

The main things that will give you most bang for your buck when it comes to music theory is to learn:

- What a scale or key is
- What notes and chords are in a scale
- How to make a chord

Now those three things might seem daunting right now, but they will help you learn almost any song out there and give you the freedom to play how and what you want. At first it will just be memorizing, but once you apply it to a song, it will allow you so much musical freedom. Just by knowing what chord you are playing at a given moment allows you almost infinite options to play harmonies and back up the melody or singer.

When I was just learning music, I wasn't taught music theory. I would practice and practice a song each note at a time. Eventually I would learn the song, and I found that I had often memorized the whole song note by note. There isn't anything wrong with this, but it was very slow learning. It was hard to take the things I memorized from that song and put it into any other song. If I had learned some basic music theory first, I would have learned everything from my four years of high school in a single year easily. This is why learning how it works together helps you learn more things faster.

Memorize some Sheet Music

Now, as I mentioned earlier, sheet music isn't the same as music theory. If music was the new language you are now learning, then sheet music would be the alphabet and way of writing that language down. I know that many musicians won't need to use sheet music that often in their practice, but I would strongly urge most people to learn the basics. It has so many benefits that the time it takes to learn the basics seems very small with the comparison of what you will get out of it. Once again, we have some key points of sheet music in the back of the book.

Learning how the notes on sheet music look on your instrument may allow you to utilize your sheet music more quickly and effectively.

The musicians that I meet, who mostly boast about how they don't know a single thing about sheet music, remind me of one of my high school teachers. He would talk about how he didn't know anything about computers and didn't even know how to turn on a computer. Yes, you can get many things done without a computer, but sending an email is a much faster way of communicating than a written letter. In the same way, learning how to read some basic sheet music can save you so much time, instead of needing to find someone who can play it for you. At the end of the day, learning sheet music allows you the freedom to learn more music without the help of someone who learned it for you.

"Learn how to see. Realize that everything connects to everything else."
Leonardo Da Vinci

Use This Tested Method to Memorize Anything

So how do you do that? This is the exact three step method you need to use.

1. **Say it out loud.**

    a. Studies show that when you say things out loud, they stick in your mind better

2. **Write it out again by HAND.**

    a. Typing things out isn't good enough you, Do Not Just Type It Out, you need to write it out long hand

3. Read it 3 times

a. Do this 3 times in a row right before bed and then again when you wake up

I'm just kidding, there is no perfect method for learning things. It's possible that some of those methods above might work. I'm sure they will work for some, but that is where the problem is "isn't it?" We don't all learn the same way. Some learn simply by reading it and memorizing it; others need tricks and pictures to learn it. You are going to memorize this information in the same way you learn many other things. Take some time to think about how you learn best.

Yes, you will find there is more than one way to memorize things.

When I started piano lessons, I also started learning sheet music. I won't lie about it; it was not my strong suit. In fact, I was bad at it. Eventually I started to get it one day and found that I didn't learn the names of the notes on sheet music (A, B, C, D, Etc.) I actually was learning where each note on the sheet music was as it pertained to a note on the piano. If I needed to say the name of the note, I had to think about what the name of the note on the piano was. It was a lot of extra steps my mind needed to take. I didn't think about the name and actually had trouble remembering them all. I remembered an image of where each note was on the keyboard. After many years and several different instruments, I no longer see the notes that way, but it helped me out a lot at the beginning. It was just how I learned it, and I have found that many students need to learn sheet music in different ways as well.

Whether you find the information on my website, or back of the book, or look it up some other way, you will need to get it in your mind and learn it.

There are a few different types of learners out there. Here are some basic examples, but you could find entire books about each type of learner if you wanted to go down that path. Start by just figuring out what type of learner you are.

Analytical Learners

If you are an analytical learner, you probably know the way that you learn best and how to memorize this type of material. Lucky for you, there is a lot of very well put together information about most parts of music. Now that you have a good understanding of what you need to find, learning it shouldn't be a problem. I have found that most of my students who learn this way usually have varying degrees of difficulty transferring that knowledge to their instruments. If that sounds like an issue you have had, then try to always physically play all the things you are trying to learn, so that it transfers from the beginning. Don't just run as far as you can memorizing everything about music. If you don't start getting it into your body, you can feel like you are behind before you even start. We will talk more about that in the next chapter on muscle memory.

Visual Learners

Many people are visual learners. For these people, they need only to look for the patterns and, the good news for them, music is full of patterns and shapes. You can learn the scales from the pattern of the circle of fifths or learn the chords on a guitar from the shape or "constellations" that they form. There are a few things like the circle of fifths that are set up easier for visual learners, but often each student will start seeing those shapes and patterns that they draw for themselves and that they remember the best. Another great thing for visual learners is the vast amount of video content that we have available. Now that you know what to search for, you can easily find those things and see someone doing it exactly.

Learn from your instrument

As I told you earlier, I learned sheet music based on the piano and not off the notes that most people name it by. In the same way, you can learn a lot of this information specifically with your instrument. This often can help you learn the info faster but also allow you to use it much quicker in your music practice. This is closely related to visual learning.

Learn the Best Way for You

No matter how you cut it up, you need to learn it the way that is best for you. Don't worry what others will say or what other people think is the right way to learn it. In the end, it is for only one purpose. It is to help you learn, and express your music. If it is accomplishing that, then it is the right way for you.

But I Don't Want To Memorize!

Well, you have to. There is no way around it. You will either memorize it on purpose or you will memorize it through practice anyway. Through repetition you will inevitably memorize many things. This chapter is about learning the most right now, and memorizing certain things to start will help you out at the beginning.

One of the reasons I have often taught music theory, and had students memorize things like notes in a key, is because it makes it so they don't have to think about other things. In some ways, we memorize things because we can't process everything at once. As an example, there are only twelve notes in western music. Most songs only play in one key and there are only seven notes in each key. So if you know what key you are playing in, you only have to think about seven notes now. If you were starting to play piano for the first time and had a keyboard with 88 keys on it, you may feel overwhelmed that you need to memorize 88 different notes. In that same way, most modern songs only play about four root chords. If I am playing in a specific key, I know that I will mostly be playing those 4 chords, and I don't have to think about every chord that there is in existence.

By memorizing some of these things, we can save time in playing because we no longer need to think about them. Learning these things will save you time, in the same way, knowing how to make a certain meal saves time, rather than needing to look at the recipe every step.

Exercise #1
Figure out how you learn

Everyone learns in different ways; so what way do you learn best?

How have you learned best in the past?

Do you need to see someone do it first?

Do you need to see it on a chart?

Do you need to physically do something before you learn it?

Think back on different things that you have learned in the past and figure out what methods you learned best from.

Exercise #2
Pick One Thing.

Pick one thing about the instrument you wish to learn or music theory by itself and start learning it today. (If you can't think of anything, then learn the notes of the C scale and how they look on sheet music)

Many people can get in a theoretical learning loop, and this step isn't part of it. This is an action step towards learning your instrument. It could be as simple as learning the notes of the strings on your guitar or how to tune your instrument. Look it up now and start to memorize it. If you don't have an instrument, then go to the store and actually go touch one.

Exercise #3
What have you learned?

(Audiobook friendly) Think right now, and through the rest of your day, of all the things you already have memorized. Passwords, the route to work or school, the way to the bathroom at night in the dark. There are so many things that we have memorized in our day to day lives. Over the years you have learned each and every one of these things. Learning music is no different, and this should give you assurance that with time you will learn music too.

Recap

Although memorizing things may not be the most fun thing about music, it is very helpful and necessary. Memorizing some things about music is building the foundation of music that you can work off of. A few things you should memorize are:

Learning the basics of your instrument

Learning the basics of Music Theory

Learning the basics of Sheet Music

These things are what you need to start memorizing, and now that you know how you learn best, we can start applying them to music through muscle memory.

Affirmation Statement

Belief:

What you believe will shape how you learn and how far you will go. Believing that you can learn music is more important than your talent, connections, or background.

If you have a desire to learn music, that is proof in itself that you have the ability to learn it.

If you maintain your belief that you can learn music as you work towards your goals, you will continually be making progress towards them.

Goals:

There are infinite things you can learn in music, and your personal goals will allow you to learn what is relevant to you. They will help you make progress towards what is meaningful to you personally. Goals that are based on emotional health and desire will make it more likely that you will continue learning and allow for your music to become a part of your life instead of a chore.

Learn:

The majority of material that you learn will be based on the goals you have set and will continually bring you closer to those goals. Breaking up what you learn into separate sections will make you learn each quality better.

Music theory for knowledge
Sheet Music for communication
Muscle Memory for consistency
Rhythm for function
Ear Training for Optionality
And Creativity for self-expression

The style and method that you learn your instrument with should be based on how you personally learn best. Many of the things you will learn don't need to be learned while touching your instrument and can be taken with you anywhere.

Each new thing you learn allows you the opportunity to learn countless more things.

We have learned so many things in our lives already, and music is no different. Take that as assurance that you can learn what you want to in music, just as you have learned so many things in the past.

Chapter #6 Muscle Memory

"Muscle has memory. The body knows things the mind will not admit"
Louise Doughty

People often say "It's just like riding a bike." Of course, what they mean is if you have learned it once, you can easily pick it up again, even if you haven't done it for years. Now mostly this is only true of things that you actually use your body to do, and there is a reason for that. The reason is because of your muscle memory. Your body remembers how to do things without your mind needing to process it. This skill is essential for anyone who wants to learn to play an instrument. At first, when you are learning an instrument, you will feel about as uncoordinated as a 2 year old running through the house with swimming flippers on, but as you work at it your muscles will learn what needs to be done.

We have all heard phrases like "practice makes perfect" or teachers saying "practice, practice, practice." At the heart of these phrases people are talking about muscle memory. Unfortunately, there is a lot more we need to practice than just muscle memory, but it is such an important part to understand. You really need to have it as a separate section while you are learning your instrument. Even if you have a brilliant mind that can process sheet music perfectly, you still need the muscle memory to play the actual notes correctly and have your fingers do what they need to do. Once you get the muscle memory down for your instrument, you are just working on what you should play. Your fingers already know what to do; they are just waiting for instructions on what direction you want them to go in.

The same could be said for an athlete. There are specific things you need to focus on in a sports game, but good athletes have trained their bodies to know what to do. Certain actions are automatic, and they just need to start playing.

Many people have heard of the 10,000 hour rule. Essentially, it claims if you have done something for 10,000 hours, you are now considered a master of it. This, of course, has a lot to do with knowledge, but a lot of it has to do with muscle memory. If a plumber works on houses for 10,000 hours, he will immediately know if something is correct or if it is defective just by the way it feels when he puts it together. Now I don't believe you need to do 10,000 hours on your instrument to have muscle memory. Once you start working on muscle memory, you can start getting the benefits. It is one of the first things you can be working on. It's something you can do before ever learning a single note or piece of sheet music.

There are no shortcuts to muscle memory. You just have to put the reps in. Muscle memory itself is actually the shortcut to playing your instrument the way you want.

One of the best things about separating muscle memory into its own category is being able to easily start to do it on day one of learning your instrument. There are simple exercises you can work on the very first day of learning music. When I teach a new student, this is often one of the key things I will teach them and have them practice to start. It's good to start out with this because, when we just begin learning an instrument, we are learning a lot all at once. We have a lot of things our minds need to memorize and think about initially. When we are working on muscle memory exercises, we don't need to think a lot with our minds. Once we get the exercise under control, it can be very fun, and it will give you a good sense of progress right away.

"Experience is a truer guide than the words of others."
Leonardo Da Vinci

Sometimes what other people say just isn't enough. We make up so many excuses in our mind why what we believe is correct for us. I can tell people all day long that once they start doing this finger exercise that it will start feeling natural, or that this part of music theory is helpful. It is not until they try it out that they often feel the benefits.

At one point I was a segway tour guide. For those who don't know, a segway is a two wheeled self balancing scooter-like vehicle. It takes a little faith to ride it the first time because it balances itself, and you just need to stand upright and trust it. I often had to teach people how to use them, and many people were very skeptical. Even though I assured them that within five or ten minutes they would be comfortable with it, they were sure they would never get it. As we did the training and everyone started going down the sidewalk behind me, we would often run across different people walking along. We would get comments like "you're braver than me" or "looks like fun, but I could never do that." The same people I had just trained a few minutes before usually let everyone know that they just learned today and anyone can do it. It wouldn't matter what my clients said, the people on the sidewalk often didn't believe them. Sometimes you just have to do it and have the experience to believe it.

I didn't learn a lot about muscle memory from teachers growing up. It was something I discovered about music as I learned through high school. When I first started learning music, I would work and work and work on a single song. By the time that it started sounding like a song at all, I would have it memorized, and I didn't need to look at the sheet music at all. I found that I didn't have the notes or the sheet music memorized. I just had the song memorized and how it was played. My hands actually knew how to play the song automatically. As I started learning more and more songs this way, I started learning more patterns and styles. If I ran across a similar pattern or style in another song, I would learn that part so much faster than any other part of the song. Of course, the sheet music would be similar for those patterns, but it was my fingers that remembered how to play it the most. When I started teaching music, I taught my students from day one how to start getting their muscles used to playing patterns they would be using in all their songs.

Muscle IQ
How much do your muscles already know?

In many ways, learning muscle memory for your instrument is the most basic thing in music you will learn. It doesn't take any musical qualities to do. You just need to know where to start. We have been learning different muscle memories through our entire lives. We spent years of growing up learning to tie our shoes, brush our teeth, or use a fork. One of the ways to see how natural these things are is to try mixing them up and doing them with your less dominant hand. If you are right handed, try brushing your teeth with your left hand for a week. At first it will feel extremely foreign to you. It's not because you are "right handed." It's just because you don't have any muscle memory with that hand doing that action. With enough time and practice, you could get that less dominant hand to be just as comfortable as the one you have been using. Even basic things like walking down a hall in a straight line is accomplished by our body's muscles knowing how to do it.

We have needed to develop many different types of muscle memory to function everyday. From cooking our food to driving our car to work, many of our daily actions would be extremely long and difficult without muscle memory. Just think about how long it would be to type out an email or text someone if you didn't have the muscle memory to do it.

It's the combination of knowing what to do and having the muscle memory to do it that will make you good at anything. Knowing what to do just isn't enough. Just think about if you were going to go out to dinner with your partner. You are going to meet their coworkers for the first time, and you don't want to look like a fool in front of them. Eating shouldn't be a problem because you know how to do it, and you have done it thousands of times. What you didn't anticipate was that your partner's co-workers chose an Asian restaurant, and it only has chopsticks, which you haven't used since you were a kid. Even though you "know" how to use chopsticks, you definitely need to have the muscle memory to use them well. All of a sudden, this casual meal got a lot harder for you, for no other reason than the fact you don't have the muscle memory for the task at hand.

My son decided he wanted to use chopsticks for everything one day. He has used them for most of all his meals for the last year. We even got him a huge set of them for cooking with (you tend to get burned cooking with the little ones.) I don't use them as much, and when we both use them, it is very obvious to that fact. They feel clunky and silly in my hands, and they look natural and easy in his hands.

Everything we practice with muscle memory is going to become easier. We are going to want that ease as we are learning music. There are too many things to think about in music without having the memory of our muscles helping us out.

"Practice Puts Brains In Our Muscles"
Sam Snead

It's often only when you put someone in a new position that you find out how they do under pressure. Many people can't function and will quickly stop, while others might stumble along trying to keep it up or fake it. We feel uncomfortable with new things mostly because we can't rely on our body to do a lot of the work. All the work falls on our mind to carry us through, and the act of learning something new and performing a task isn't something most of us are good at when we need to do them at the same time. This is one of the reasons that muscle memory is so important.

When we complete a task over and over again, our bodies will start to do it automatically. In most cases this is necessary in the process of becoming the musician you want to be. The good thing about this is learning to get muscle memory is not a complex thing. You get muscle memory from doing any of the regular things you do everyday. You never have to think about how to sign your name. You don't need to remember how to unlock your phone. You just do them because you have worked on them every day. In the same way, we will build new muscle memory skills for your instrument. We will do the same action every day, and it will become built into our body.

You don't need a gym membership to start learning muscle memory.

I've known many people who have bought instruments and have wanted to learn. By the time they have gotten around to reaching out to me to teach them, it's been months or years since they bought the instrument, and they have barely touched it. Instruments are meant to be touched, and there are many things we can do without "knowing music" to work with them.

An easy place to start is rhythm. When I have people work on rhythm, I often don't want them to think about the notes right away. Listen to a song you enjoy and tap your knee to the rhythm of the music. 1 2 3 4, 1 2 3 4. Many people do this from time to time, but the trick is to actually think about the beat and tap along to it for the entire song. Never missing a single beat like you are on a stage and playing the song yourself. You may feel like this isn't really practice or really music, but it is the continual work of it that will get you more in tune with music. Do this with a song or two every day, and you will start to notice an effect.

You can also do it with an instrument instead. If you are playing a stringed instrument like guitar or ukulele, you can put a loose cloth over the strings on the neck of the instrument. This will dampen the sound, and it won't ring out. Now with the instrument muted, put on a song you like. Strum along with the song exactly like you are playing all the chords. Pianists who are using a keyboard can simply turn off the keyboard and press a note down with one finger at a time as the song plays. Songs are a lot longer than what people practice, and playing along with the entire song and keeping a steady rhythm can be harder than people think.

Flow

The purpose, when we start out, is to get into a flow. At the beginning, things are rarely flowing right away. We need to think about every movement, and it feels, clunky and difficult. When I was twelve years old I broke my arm. There were several things that I couldn't do at all, and everything else felt awkward. When my arm finally healed, it had been so long since I had used it, everything came slowly. I had to think specifically about how to hold and shoot a basketball. My writing was slower and deliberate. After about a week of working with it again, you wouldn't have known that it had been broken at all.

Working on muscle memory exercises allow you to get into a flow with music that many musicians strive for.

The point of working with this separately is not to learn the most about music possible. The point is to get your body to learn how to play your instrument naturally and efficiently. Your body is just making a movement and making it natural. Your body doesn't care if the movement is music or driving, it will consistently learn anything you tell it too.

Exercise #1

Pick a finger exercise for your instrument and work on it five minutes a day. This is how I start every single one of my classes with my one-on-one students. Once again, if you don't know of any or have trouble finding them, just go to the website www.speakingmusic.online and check out a few examples there.

Now this might not be possible for every instrument, but most instruments you can do the muscle memory exercises anywhere. You can get small practice 6 fret guitar necks for doing exercises and learning chords on. These are silent and can fit in your pocket. In the same way, you can get small folding keyboards and bring a piano with you anywhere. I had one that I would always bring to work when I was working in manufacturing and work on a few things on my lunch break every day. It's going to be the consistent working on it that will start to bring the results, not the price or quality of the instrument you use.

Exercise #2

Tap along to a song. I'm sure you think you have great rhythm when you are playing air drums in the car, but this will be a little more focused. I want you to tap each finger individually one at a time to the beat. 1234, 1234. If you are learning a stringed instrument, then press each finger one at a time to your thumb. If you are learning piano, then press each finger down one at a time on a flat surface. First use your left hand, then your right. Once again, this is something that you can do anywhere, and you will see the benefits from doing it over and over again.

Exercise #3

(Audiobook Friendly) Think of all the things in the day that you already do by muscle memory. You use turn signals in the car, you use a fork, and brush your teeth every day.

We do so many things by muscle memory every day. Think about everything you do throughout the day and list in your head the things you now do automatically. Parts of music will come as naturally as many of these things when you put in the repetition.

It's hard for some people to believe this, but think about brushing your teeth for a second. You only brush your teeth for a few minutes a day (maybe 5 or 6 minutes.) As far as practice goes, that does not seem like very much. Now try to use your less dominant hand for a day. It will feel awkward and out of rhythm. In the same way, your guitar strumming may not be the most consistent right now, but will become almost automatic with practice.

Recap

There isn't anything that is natural for us to do when we come into this world. When we are first born, we can't even use our hands to hold things correctly. We've learned to do things automatically by repeating those actions over and over again.

The great thing about this is that everyone has done it before. You know you can learn these physical movements because you have learned so many things like this before. There isn't anything specifically musical or related to talent when it comes to placing your finger on a piano key. It's just a movement, and it's a movement that will feel as natural as tying your shoes once you have done it enough times.

Many people wait to work on those actions till they have "learned more" about their instrument, but you shouldn't wait. You can start working on muscle memory actions starting on day one. Even with as little as 5 minutes a day, you will start to get muscle memory, just like brushing your teeth.

Affirmation Statement

Belief:

What you believe will shape how you learn and how far you will go. Believing that you can learn music is more important than your talent, connections, or background.

If you have a desire to learn music, that is proof in itself that you have the ability to learn it.

If you maintain your belief that you can learn music as you work towards your goals, you will continually be making progress towards them.

Goals:

There are infinite things you can learn in music, and your personal goals will allow you to learn what is relevant to you. They will help you make progress towards what is meaningful to you personally. Goals that are based on emotional health and desire will make it more likely that you will continue learning and allow for your music to become a part of your life instead of a chore.

Learn:

The majority of material that you learn will be based on the goals you have set and will continually bring you closer to those goals.

Breaking up what you learn into separate sections will make you learn each quality better.

Music theory for knowledge

Sheet Music for communication

Muscle Memory for consistency

Rhythm for function

Ear Training for Optionality

And Creativity for self-expression

The style and method that you learn your instrument with should be based on how you personally learn best. Many of the things you will learn don't need to be learned while touching your instrument and can be taken with you anywhere.

Each new thing you learn allows you the opportunity to learn countless more things.

We have learned so many things in our lives already, and music is no different. Take that as assurance that you can learn what you want to in music, just as you have learned so many things in the past.

Practice:

Muscle memory combines what we have learned with a simple practice, making it so that we don't have to think about each individual part of music. We can let our muscles do a lot of the work.

How you practice will be the defining difference between succeeding in learning music and not. It is something that every musician has needed to do.

Practice is something that can and should be fun and enjoyable to do. For most musicians, practice will be how they play the majority of their music.

Basic consistent practice, combined with the belief that you can learn music, will allow you to reach any goal you set.

Chapter #7 Practice

"Being willing is not enough,
we must do."
Leonardo Da Vinci

    This can be a very misunderstood area of music. Some students think that going to their half hour lesson each week is all the practice they need. Others try to do two hours a day, and when that isn't sustainable, they think they just don't have the talent to do music and quit. Many people come into lessons thinking that they will hate practicing, but they "know it's what they need to do."

    Practice is misunderstood because it involves so much of music, and so much of our time playing music. It can be many things. The trick is to make it something you enjoy and consistently do.

You don't really need to practice, just go buy another course instead.

I was on our high school basketball team, and I won't lie, we didn't win much. There were many different factors to this, but I discovered a major one in my junior year. Most of the time we would do daily practice after school and may play a little together during lunch. Someone mentioned that year that we shouldn't ever miss our free throws because no one is blocking you. You just need to shoot the ball, and all that takes is practice. We needed to shoot 10 free throws every practice. I knew for a fact that 10 free throws of practice wasn't enough for me obviously. I ended up practicing them in the morning before school and sometimes during lunch. I probably only increased my practice to about 50 free throws a day, three days a week, but the results were obvious. I probably made twice as many free throws in each game. For some reason I never took this same mentality to all the other parts of basketball. If I had, we probably would have won a few more games.

I did take this mentality to music. I wasn't taking lessons for piano during high school, and so all the practice was based on my own schedule. I would practice about a half hour before school everyday. This would usually consist of trying to learn a part of a particular song I was working on. I would also always play a couple of other songs that I knew well and enjoyed. I also decided at that time to pick up the violin. During one of my study halls at school, I would either practice more piano or violin.

It wasn't until I started teaching music, in my early twenties, that the importance of practice became really apparent. I found that talent didn't play a very large role in learning music. It made practicing easier, but it didn't define who learned music and who gave up. From four year olds to eighty year olds, from talented or not, guitar or violin, the thing that seemed to make people progress and learn music or not was practice.

A continual thing I saw in my students was their beliefs. A teenager who was talented would make a lot of progress all at once. They had confidence and knew they could do it. In fact, it was easy for them. They would be excited about learning, and then one day they would hit a wall. It could be anything. They may not have been able to remember certain notes in a scale or consistently play a rhythm. Usually they would hit a wall by not being able to complete a song they wanted to learn. Instead of trying to push through by working on certain parts or methods to learn a song, they would start to believe that they weren't good enough. These students often didn't have a great practice routine anyway. Why would they need to? It was always easy for them, and armed with their new belief that they couldn't do it, they would inevitably lose motivation completely. If they had worked through it, they would have probably come out again on the other side finding it easy and progressing again, but their belief changed. When they stopped practicing, they would stop learning music.

A lot of students, especially those who weren't as talented, would need a while to start to believe they could become a musician at all. Through practice and through showing them that they were learning music they would start to form that belief. Like everyone else, these students would hit a wall from time to time and have a hard time progressing at a certain point. It wasn't some secret knowledge I gave them, it was usually continual practice and trying out slightly different perspectives that would allow them to break through. The students with the best practice routines always went the furthest and seemed to enjoy it the most.

What is practice, really?

For most people practice is a means to an end. It's the pain in the phrase "no pain no gain." It's the real price you have to pay to enjoy playing music like you know you will someday. When people find out I am a music teacher, they often say things like, " I used to take piano when I was younger, I remember my teacher making me practice my scales." They would roll their eyes like it was such a painful thing they needed to do.

At the end of the day, most musicians play music that we would call "practice" ten times more than they would ever play in a "performance." Many musicians won't ever play a gig in their life. They enjoy playing music for themselves. It's relaxing, calming, and it helps them think clearer. So where is the line for them? Are they always practicing or are they always performing for themselves?

I have done many jobs in my life, and some of them have been physically taxing. It wasn't until I was in my late twenties I heard a thought process and tried it out. The thought was this, if you need to do physical work at a job, you should switch your mindset while you are doing it to "This is my exercise for the day." If I was lifting something over and over again, I would think, "Wow, I can really feel this in my arms. It's like a full arm workout for the day." That simple change in thought would make it seem less tiring and sometimes energizing to do. In the same way, practice is a mindset that you control yourself.

We often think about practice today in a weird light. We view it as separate from the performance or arriving where you want. We don't ever arrive in the end. We are always either growing or losing ground. It's working on our music over and over that allows us to continue to grow. It's the practice that "is" our music. It's important to find as much of that practice time as you can to be enjoyable. That practice is going to make up most of the time you ever play your instrument (for most people.) Think of music like learning a new language. Once you get a basic hold of the language, you will spend most of your time practicing how to speak it. You will do this by listening to others and speaking it yourself. You won't be spending most of your time practicing how to speak so you can go up and give a big speech to lots of people. That may be needed from time to time, but mostly you will just be using it day to day in a normal way. Practice. You wouldn't practice speaking the language for a year and then be done. I'll just practice speaking that language a little bit before I have to give a big speech. You would use that language whenever you had a chance.

This is why it is so important to enjoy practice. Practice is music. From the first time you set your fingers to your instrument, you are playing music. You will just become a better musician as you play it more. Many people are just so overwhelmed by learning an instrument at first, that they can't even relax enough to enjoy the music they are making. From day one, there are things you can play that can be enjoyable. This is one of the reasons I separate the different parts of learning music. Aspects of music, like learning sheet music, are basically just memorizing and people don't often find that enjoyable on day one. Separating sheet music from finger exercises or rhythm exercises makes it easier to identify what things you enjoy more easily.

"You are what you do, not what you say you'll do."
Carl Jung

Doesn't Make You Perfect

There is a crucial moment you will come to when learning music. That moment is when you say and believe that you are a musician. I can tell you that all people can be musicians, and you were the moment you sang a song as a kid or decided you wanted to learn an instrument, but that isn't the same thing. What I say doesn't matter. What matters is the moment you believe it. Practice doesn't make you perfect, because perfect is an end. Music doesn't have an end. Practice does make you better, and better is something you can attain every day. Better is what we are always working towards.

There was a year, when I was 22, that my wife and I were in fourteen different weddings. Some she was in and I was in others. I was playing music for many of them. Almost all of the ones I played for, I ended up playing a version of Pachebell's Canon. For the first wedding, I thought I learned the song perfectly. I was wrong. I played it so many different ways by the end of the year, it actually changed from being a performance to something that I practiced with. I could play around with it in a new way and change it up on demand. It became such a fun song to practice with after that because I knew it so much better. The more I learned about it, the more I found that I could learn more about it. You will find this in most aspects of music.

If you look at practice as part of the enjoyment of playing music, and not just a step that you have to take, you will open up an entire new source of enjoyment for yourself. There are some people who I would teach that would learn a finger exercise and always try to play it as fast as they could. They would just stumble along, way faster than they should constructively play, so they could show how much they "knew" the finger exercise and try to get that part of the music lessons over with. The students who could accept that it could be a fun part of music I would end up doing more with. We would combine learning a new chord pattern or new scale with the finger exercise. Sometimes we would take a rhythm from one of the songs they were learning and attach that to the finger exercise. When something finally clicked, and they started to really get the new rhythm, they would just light up.

Once we start enjoying something, learning it will progress faster. For most people, they need to "start" enjoying it at some point. There is so much to learn at first that often it doesn't feel enjoyable to people right off the bat. You need to learn so much that your brain takes up all the energy you have. This is why you should break up your practice into different sections. I've mentioned these in previous chapters. I break it up into: Music Theory, Sheet Music, Muscle Memory, Rhythm, Ear Training, and Creativity. Depending on your learning style, you will most likely be better at one section or another. You should focus a little extra time on the section you are better at. Just play around with it and feel some enjoyment from it.

 Practice can be one of the most rewarding parts of music. It is also one of the things you will spend the most of your time on. Allow yourself to enjoy this and learn to feel the music.

When you start to get really comfortable with something, it gets easier and easier to play with it and enjoy it. This enjoyment will eventually turn into you loving to do it. Once we love something, the practice almost always takes care of itself. It isn't thought of as a chore anymore. It is something we look forward to. You may think, "It's hard to love practicing scales, Micah." At the beginning, it might be because you don't know it well, but it won't stay that way. As you know more about music and learn more songs, you will see different parts of your practice right in the songs you already listen too. In a section of Canon in D, you play up all seven notes of the key you are playing in, just like you are practicing your scale. It doesn't feel like practicing because you are hearing the music of the song and not an exercise. You can do the same thing with any of your music exercises. Find the music in the exercise, and they won't be just exercises anymore.

"You should not give up, unless you are forced to give up"
Elon Musk

What are your goals?

A lot of what you will practice will come down to what your goals are. How you practice will change quite a bit based on those goals. You may say that you want to learn a certain song. That is not very specific though. I could learn many songs within five or ten minutes, if my goal for that song was to just enjoy playing it for myself without needing to memorize it or anything. If I planned to play that with a band in front of hundreds of people I will need to practice it quite differently.

Let's say you wanted to learn a certain song really well, but mostly for yourself. Some of your practice will have to do with learning about the song itself. What key is it in? What chords does it have? What repeating patterns does it have? Once you find out some of these things you can put them into your practice. Your scale or chords you practice will be the ones from that song. When you work on muscle memory or finger exercises, you will pick a rhythm from that song. After you worked on a few of the basic practices, then you can put them together and work on the actual song itself.

Almost every practice that I set up for people has four main parts to it.

- Tune Your Instrument
- Work on Music Theory
- Work on Muscle Memory
- Work on a Song

These four things can incorporate a lot of things. We typically already know what song they are going to work on, and that is where most everything starts. We will work on chords or scales from that song to focus on music theory. We will typically pick a rhythm that is part of the song and work on our muscle memory from that. By the time we get to the song, they are so prepped that they learn much more of it than they would've if we had just jumped right into the song by itself.

I've shown you in previous chapters how breaking up learning into different sections helps you learn better. You don't need to learn all of the sheet music and rhythm at the same time. When you are practicing your song, you don't need to practice it all at once. If you are learning the chords to the song, then you could have the song playing or hum along the tune and just play the chords without worrying about the rhythm. Alternately, I can practice just the rhythm of a song. You can do this with a guitar by putting a piece of fabric like a towel over the strings to mute them and just work on strumming without worrying about the chords. With a keyboard, you can have the song playing and work on the rhythm with the keyboard off, so you don't focus on the notes but just the rhythm.

 Breaking up the songs and working on rhythm and notes separately can speed up the progress.

Breaking up a song will have the same benefits as breaking up the rest of music. You can try learning an entire song all at once, but even if it's not a train wreck, it won't be thoroughly learned as if you break it up. If you are practicing a scale at the time, make sure it's the scale that the song you are playing is in. Work on that one exclusively for a while. When you are working on a rhythm exercise, take a rhythm from the song you are learning and put that into your exercise. If you are practicing some chords, then take the chords from the song and work on those.

What you have done at this point is taken the first half of your practice and done prep work for your song. When you start working on your song, it will feel more natural. Your fingers will already be used to the rhythm and chords of the song. This will make it so much nicer to learn the song.

Consistency is the Key

Knowing exactly what to learn is great. Knowing what your goals are is also necessary. Having a lot of talent will make learning faster. One thing, more than anything else, will decide if you get better at music or not, and that is consistency of practice. I know it's not earth shattering to hear that, and it's not the sexiest method, but it's true. It's one of the reasons that weekly music lessons with a teacher are so productive. Knowing that you will need to keep practicing, because your teacher will be asking what you've done, is half the benefits of lessons.

The main reason I progressed with learning piano during my high school years was because I practiced everyday before school for about a half hour. This started out as convenience and ended up turning into a habit. There were a lot of kids in my family, and in order to get in the shower before school, I would get up earlier than everyone else. This worked out great, and I would be ready for school about a half hour early and would be waiting for everyone else. I started practicing my piano during that time. Even as more of my siblings graduated and left the house, I kept up the routine because it had become a habit by then.

It wasn't that I had this extra time all of a sudden. That wasn't the key at all. It was the fact that I never had to think about when I would practice. I always did it at the same time everyday. Having a consistent time everyday that you practice will be more beneficial than practicing for a longer time once a week. This is especially true at the beginning. Your finger and body need consistent time to get that muscle memory in. I was a normal kid though, and since my routine was to practice before school, guess how much I practiced during the summer? Not very much.

You don't need to do it in the morning like I did. It doesn't actually matter what time of day, as long as it is consistent. A good trick to making this consistent is to make a specific time and place you can trigger this practice. Something like " After I put my dishes in the dishwasher after supper, I will tune my guitar or play one scale on the piano." (If you are the type of person who knows they should put their dishes in the dishwasher but end up just putting them in the sink that is fine too.)

Why would just tuning your instrument or playing a single scale make such a big difference? First it will make a big difference because it is a much easier habit to make. The act of tuning your instrument or playing a scale may only take two minutes or so. Everyone has time in their day for that. The next reason is that it will not end up being just tuning the instrument. Once you are used to getting your instrument out everyday you will think, " As long as I have it out, I should really try playing this song." It will be a fun time to play around with your instrument and not an arduous task of "practicing" everyday.

Not a chore

It is not easy to learn music if you view your practice time as a chore. There are a lot of things that need to be learned right off and viewing it as a chore can be very intimidating. Practice is the very start of you learning music. It can be exciting. It can be broken down into simple things that you can play on your very first day. That means you can start playing music on your very first day. Getting into some of the exercises and practice can be fun and enjoyable. Don't turn it into something that you won't enjoy.

It will, of course, depend on your goals in music but for most people they will mostly be practicing music. Some people end up playing music professionally. They may play in a wedding band or at the bar in town. After they have learned a song very well and have played it over and over again, they may not need to practice as much. For most people, even if they are performing in front of others, they will end up practicing much more than they ever perform. Other musicians will mostly play for themselves or close friends and family their whole lives. In the end, what most musicians do is practice. So it stands to reason that, when you find a musician who enjoys playing music, you will find that they enjoy practicing music.

After you have played for a certain time, some things will become more automatic, and it's getting into that flow that many people really enjoy as musicians. I have found that most curriculums and ways to start learning music don't have a place for this at the beginning. It's all memorizing and drills. Many people get depressed from doing these things, and they end up giving up because they don't see the progress. That is why breaking up your learning into different sections like muscle memory and rhythm can be so beneficial. You can learn some exercises that allow you to get into that flow and really enjoy it.

Are We There Yet?

I often get a question from my students that has to do with how long it will take to learn their instrument or to learn music. It isn't easy to answer that question because, as you learn your instrument more, you find that there is always more to learn about music and about your instrument. There isn't an end, so it's hard to say how long it will take. A lot of this comes back to your goal. If you want to learn a song so you can play guitar for an open mic, then it won't take as long as becoming a professional pianist for an esteemed orchestra.

For almost everything you learn there is a pattern of learning or a learning curve. When you first get information, you are trying to process it all. There is often a period of just memorization where you are putting meaning behind the new words you are learning. After that, there is a period of organization where you are learning to use that information and, it starts to become more natural. This is where muscle memory steps in. As you use the information, your body starts to create muscle memory and habits that we don't think about. This goes back and forth as we learn more and as we apply that knowledge. We start to get a broader understanding and certain types of things we can learn more quickly. The second or third instruments you learn are much easier to learn than your first one because of this reason.

 When you start practicing something new for the first time, record that practice. It will be horrible. Your timing will be off. You will hit the wrong notes. Then record that same exercise or song after you have practiced it for a month. This will show you all the great progress you have made.

When I was in high school, I got my first official job. It was at a coffee shop. My first day on the job, about all I did was learn how much cream and sugar went into the different size cups and how to make the coffee. I had made coffee before in my life, but all the equipment was different, and the orders came fast. Over the next year, I learned more and more about the job - from making the muffins and bagels to cleaning the machines. It got to a point that, when I got to work, I could almost immediately see what needed to be done for my shift the second I walked in.

The same principle goes for learning music. At first you are just figuring out how to put your fingers on the strings of your instrument so they sound right. Later you can play with other people and know exactly what needs to be played to fill in the sound best. That journey takes different amounts of time for different people.

Once again, the majority of time playing music will be "practice. It's worth the time to learn how to practice in a fun and pleasing way. Like all things, of course, sometimes you just won't feel like doing it. Other times, you will have a very hard time learning a certain thing. Everything we do in life has its ups and downs. You have to enjoy the journey. Know that, when you are having a hard time you will get through it, and you will enjoy it all the more when you have that difficulty turned into muscle memory and a habit.

Exercise #1
Fun Practice

Everything starts small and we are going to start with one exercise. Pick one music warmup or exercise that you can enjoy doing. If you haven't started your instrument yet, you will have to start by looking up exercises to do.

Once you have decided on a single exercise that you like, start playing it a little longer. Think of it as no longer an exercise, but as a piece of music that you are playing. Don't think about it as being played right or wrong; just play around with it. This is not only the first step in learning your instrument better, but also improvisation and creativity.

Exercise #2
Pick a song

Take a song you are learning or want to learn. Break it down to one section and practice that section separately. You could take the rhythm part of the song and work on just the rhythm. You could just take the melody and work on just that. Working on breaking down the song into different parts will help you listen and learn the song better just in that step. Practicing those parts will make you learn the song better as a whole and help you progress.

Exercise #3
Make Time

(Audiobook Friendly)Think of all the times that you could practice your music. The most important part of practice is consistency. One of the ways of forming habits is both picking the time and place to do something. So if you think that at the end of the day is a good time to practice, you may want to make that more specific. Instead of thinking, "I'll practice after work," you could decide to tune your guitar after you put your keys away when you get home from work. Or you could decide to play one scale after you put your dirty dishes away after supper every night.

Having decided when and where you will practice will make those decisions easier and eventually automatic. Making a decision on where and when to practice will be a crucial step for learning any instrument.

Recap

If you have the desire to learn music, then you can definitely learn it. That belief is very important in every step of music but especially when it comes to practice. Mindless and heartless practice, to please your parents or make your teacher happy, isn't going to be as effective at all as practice with a purpose. Knowing that you are doing what you need to do to reach your goals, is very powerful. Hold that thought in your mind, and you will grow rapidly.

Practice is necessary. Things take time. It's through the repetition of anything that we get comfortable with it and eventually make it automatic. Finding a time to practice everyday can be the difference between learning music or not. Even if it's just playing some chords or scales, having some time every day that you work on your music will create a drastic effect in the long run.

Practicing by itself is playing music and it's fun. This is probably one of the most important steps for the enjoyment of music. Getting to a place where the things you need to practice are also enjoyable, and you can enjoy the music you create when you are practicing, is a great accomplishment. It allows you to more sustainably learn and practice while, at the same time, get the benefits of creating music.

Many people work on learning something new and get into a learning loop or cycle. They get another book about the subject. They listen to another podcast or video on it. They find out this or that method. This is any type of learning; it isn't just music. It can often be that the skill and habit they are learning is nothing more than learning. If you don't take the time to actually play the music, or write the song, or go to that open mic, then you won't really be learning music. You will just be learning how you should learn music. If you find that you are caught in this loop, then start by learning something today that you can practice. Take one of the exercises in the book and actually finish it. Start on that first actual step to learning music.

Affirmation Statement

Belief:

What you believe will shape how you learn and how far you will go. Believing that you can learn music is more important than your talent, connections, or background.

If you have a desire to learn music, that is proof in itself that you have the ability to learn it.

If you maintain your belief that you can learn music as you work towards your goals, you will continually be making progress towards them.

Goals:

There are infinite things you can learn in music, and your personal goals will allow you to learn what is relevant to you. They will help you make progress towards what is meaningful to you personally. Goals that are based on emotional health and desire will make it more likely that you will continue learning and allow for your music to become a part of your life instead of a chore.

Learn:

The majority of material that you learn will be based on the goals you have set and will continually bring you closer to those goals. Breaking up what you learn into separate sections will make you learn each quality better.

Music theory for knowledge
Sheet Music for communication
Muscle Memory for consistency
Rhythm for function
Ear Training for Optionality
And Creativity for self-expression

The style and method that you learn your instrument with should be based on how you personally learn best. Many of the things you will learn don't need to be learned while touching your instrument and can be taken with you anywhere.

Each new thing you learn allows you the opportunity to learn countless more things.

We have learned so many things in our lives already, and music is no different. Take that as assurance that you can learn what you want to in music, just as you have learned so many things in the past.

Practice:

Muscle memory combines what we have learned with a simple practice, making it so that we don't have to think about each individual part of music. We can let our muscles do a lot of the work.

How you practice will be the defining difference between succeeding in learning music and not. It is something that every musician has needed to do.

Practice is something that can and should be fun and enjoyable to do. For most musicians, practice will be how they play the majority of their music.

Basic consistent practice, combined with the belief that you can learn music, will allow you to reach any goal you set.

Chapter #8 Sharing

"If you only have a hammer you tend to see every problem as a nail."
Abraham Maslow

Sharing is a natural part of learning. You wouldn't be able to learn anything about music, that you didn't make yourself, if others didn't share it with you. People and things teach you all the time. It doesn't matter if they know they are doing it or not. Some people do really well in a traditional music teacher setting, and some people don't. In this chapter, we are going to go over what you may want to look for in a music teacher and ways to become a better musician by sharing what you know with others. Playing a song you learned for your partner is the same act as me writing this book. It is just normal people sharing with others what they have learned, in the knowledge that it will help them.

I had a few different teachers over the years. My first one was my mother. She was an elementary school teacher and played piano for our church sometimes. She taught me some basic sheet music and got me some music to play. "If you get a good handle on the basics you can learn anything." That was essentially her teaching style for music and elementary school. It is a very solid teaching basis and helps a lot of people. After a couple of years of just practicing, I felt I wanted to learn more.

I convinced my parents to let me take piano lessons once a week. For the next two years, I took piano lessons from a very good pianist. Her teaching style was pretty much "practice makes perfect." I was twelve, at the time, and pretty much did what teachers and adults told me to do. After a couple years I decided that I was going to keep practicing every week anyway and didn't need to continue lessons at that time. I made the hard choice at fourteen to stop lessons, which is essentially firing my piano teacher. I decided to keep practicing and learn more on my own.

Those were my first two teachers, and over those years, I learned a lot. I didn't know what I wanted from them or from music at that time. What type of ten year old does? If you can know what you want to learn already, you can learn it much faster, and that is what I started to learn from my high school years as I explored different aspects of both music and myself.

You are going to find that as you look for a music teacher (if you decide to get a music teacher) they are all very different. They all have their pros and cons based on what you are looking for. Some will be flexible, and some just see you as another nail and their system as the hammer.

"Thinking is difficult, that is why most people judge."
Carl Jung

There are many different thoughts on music, and as you start to learn, you will find that people are very willing to tell you what they think.

"If you just learn sheet music, you'll be great; I know I should've done that."

"You will do great; I can see you have big hands for it."

"Don't get your hopes up because most people don't make it in music."

"You shouldn't start charging for your music till you are better."

"Don't put your music online, or people will steal it and claim it as their own."

"You need to learn these songs first, or you won't have a foundation to work off of."

I wouldn't tell you to disregard what most people say, but only view what they say as coming from them. Most people (even your personal music teacher) often have a very one sided view on music. It's just the way they learned it. Because they don't have a very rounded view of it, their advice is very limited and specific. Most people don't have a very good understanding about who you are either. Even close friends and family members probably don't know what your plans are with music or how you learn best. So don't take too much stock in what people tell you about learning music. If you take the advice and do the lessons in this book, you will know more of what you should learn about music, for you personally, than almost anyone else.

Belief Can be Difficult

The first step to learning something is to believe that you can learn it. This can be a little confusing to people for a lot of reasons. We have many different views on who can learn music in our society. Many people think only a select few who are talented can learn music. Many people have tried to learn and didn't have the success they thought they would have. Other people have had family members or friends tell them they would or wouldn't be good at learning music.

It's important to put these doubts aside from your mind and know that if you have a desire to learn music, then you can do it. There are so many things in life you have already learned, and this is just one more thing that you can definitely do. This is probably the most important job of the music teacher. Your music teacher should be constantly reinforcing this thought. Unfortunately this can also be a double edged sword. I have worked with many people who had huge hangups about certain parts of music (usually voice related) because a teacher had told them they wouldn't be good at this or that.

Having a good teacher can be so beneficial for this purpose. They have seen so many go through all the stages you are going through in learning music. They can easily see the progress you are making and show you how much you have improved. Many people, who try to teach themselves, can't see their own improvement as much and become discouraged. There are definitely ways to overcome this, if you are teaching yourself, but having a teacher is a great way to help you in your belief that you can do it.

What a Teacher Is and Isn't

People often view music teachers as either one of two things - A good teacher or a bad teacher. Of course, this is true, to an extent, but it is infinitely more complicated than this. There are different music methods for learning an instrument. Some teachers may just use one method only, and that may not work for some students. As we have talked about briefly in this book, the Speaking Music Method is about Belief, Goals, Learning, Practice, and

Sharing. It is a little different from other methods in that it is more of a learning style and can also adopt other methods along with it. You can learn a different style of music and still work through it by breaking it up into those sections.

Learning what you want and need out of music will get you so much further along when looking for a teacher. Your relationship with them will be smooth and functional.

On top of music methods that you find, there are just different teaching styles. Some music teaching styles are more structured, while others are much more relaxed and flexible. Some styles of teaching work with absolutes of right or wrong and pass and fail, while others work with progressive improvement. None of the styles of teaching are right or wrong. They are the perfect style for certain students. The trick is to find the right match up of students and teachers. It is also helpful if the teacher can change his style based on the student.

I was teaching at a music studio once, and we had several different style music teachers. Most of them were very basic guitar teachers. This was perfect because most of the students who came through were looking for exactly that. Then there was me, and I had quite a different style. I taught piano, guitar, and voice at this studio, and I came at it through a beta version of the Speaking Music Method. I approached it with a relaxed style but backed with music theory and based on what the student wanted. There was another piano and voice teacher in the studio. She was an older Russian lady, and our styles were almost opposite. She was strict. She did exactly the same thing for each student and had people bring homework home. We got along fine, but our approaches were very different.

One day, I got a new student who wanted to learn piano. I sat down with her and went over some basic things. I showed her a basic finger exercise and had her repeat it. She kept asking questions that she was worrying about like, "Shouldn't we be learning sheet music first?" and "Shouldn't we have a book we are working out of?" When I first meet a student, there is always a point of decision for me. Are the tendencies of this student what they need for learning, or are they just limiting beliefs that we can work through? When we got to the point in the class where we wanted to work on a song, I asked her what song she would want to learn. She looked like she was going to die from anxiety. She couldn't believe for a second that a song that she picked could be the "correct" song to start with. I knew right then and there that I could modify my entire teaching to work with this girl, or I could just have her work with the Russian lady down the hall and they would both have a blast. Knowing what style is needed and finding that in a teacher will be very helpful to how you can learn. I went with the latter, and she switched over to the Russian lady and did great.

> *"If you can't explain it simply, You don't understand it well enough."*
> *Albert Einstein*

Music teachers are just normal people who are teaching you what they have learned. They are going to have all the differences within themselves that any musicians will have. There are so many types of music now and so many goals that musicians have, that we need to have an equal number of different types of teaching styles. This means, that if you want to find a teacher that works for you, then you will need to know what you want and find someone who will teach you that way.

Music teachers don't have the full authority on music. It is very difficult to find many absolutes in music at all. Of course, if you are playing a C scale, and you hit a note that isn't in the C scale, your teacher will say "That note isn't in the scale. Let's try it again this way." Many parts of music theory are well defined, but how to play music is limitless. There are infinite ways to play and equally infinite ways to learn. There is no right or wrong way to start. Again,most of this will now come down to what you want to learn. You can learn anything in music, and you can go as far as you want. You will have to learn in different ways based on those goals. You don't have to feel bad if you start learning from someone and then find that it isn't the right fit for you. They are probably the perfect fit for someone else, and you can definitely find someone who is a good fit for you and your goals at this time of your life.

If you are looking for a music teacher, you don't need to start with looking at the teachers and see what they offer. You need to start by looking at yourself and deciding what you need. No matter how good the music teacher is, you are not going to get good results by going to a music studio and just asking to get lessons learning music. You will get better results if you know what you want and ask specifically for that. "I don't know how to play guitar, but I would like to learn how to play my husband's favorite song for his birthday in three months." This request is much more likely to get you what you want, than leaving it up to the teacher to decide the pace.

The next thing that will help you pick a teacher best for you is knowing how you learn, like we talked about earlier. If you need specific assignments and homework, then you shouldn't choose a laid back, beach vibes, guitar teacher. You may feel like they are not putting in the effort you expect, when really they are teaching from a style that doesn't work for you. So going back over what style of learning works for you, and what teaching style fits that, will save you time, money, and a lot of wasted effort.

Remember, you can learn music. The fact that you want to will show that you have the ability inside you. Give yourself the best chance of expressing that by figuring out what you want to learn or get from music and then, if you go forward in that direction, finding a teacher that will help you accomplish it.

"You can learn anything you want for free"
Elon Musk

Good Teachers are Indispensable.

I am a notorious DIYer. Those things have ranged from home additions, to music, and even to fixing and living on a boat for several years with my wife and kids. Most of that stuff I learned for free. I even had some great teachers that taught me for free. I helped them with something, and they helped me with something else. The truth of the matter is that if I can find a good teacher, when I am learning something new, I learn it better and faster. I just can't always find a good teacher.

See Gaps in Music

When I first start working with a new student, I run through a lot of things in those first few lessons. I do this to see what they know and what they have been exposed to. I can usually see things that they haven't worked on at all or things that they haven't heard of. Depending on what their goals are, they may not need those things, but normally, it shows me what we need to focus on. We all learn at different speeds, and sometimes certain parts of music will come easier to us than others. When I break up practicing and learning music into the different categories - rhythm, creativity, muscle memory, or sheet music: I can see what things the student is good at and what they have already learned. It's great when someone can soar ahead in a certain area, but we need to also build up the other areas so they can continue to grow. This is definitely possible to do on your own, but is much easier to find out from a teacher. That outside perspective often can see the gaps in your practice that you can't see on your own.

Move Through Blockages

This is a common problem with most people. We run into something that we can't seem to get through. It's really a normal problem with most aspects of our life, but it applies to music also. It could be any part of music. For some reason, we work at it and can't seem to progress in a certain area. A good teacher will typically have more perspective and see different options to try. When we are learning on our own, we tend to face this problem from one angle and then get the same negative effect over and over again. I have known people who have had a really hard time with rhythm and stress over it, but figure out, in the end, that they need to work on learning their chords. Their rhythm was off because they were thinking about how to play the next chord. Seeing what the issue is can speed up your learning, and make it fun again, if you have been frustrated with a blockage you are experiencing.

Once you can move through these blockages, people often feel like they reached that breakthrough they were looking for. It doesn't always happen, but you will notice it a lot more often when working with a good teacher, than continually working on the same thing yourself year after year.

Give Affirmations

Often when we are working on learning music by ourselves, it is difficult to see how far we have come. I know, for myself, once I learn something, it feels like I have always known it. It can be hard to see the progress that I've made. If you have a bad week or find a certain thing hard to learn, it can be very demoralizing. One of the things that a good teacher can do is easily see how far you have come and let you know your progress. One of the main things that keep people learning is seeing they are making progress and enjoying what they are doing. It doesn't seem like much, but having someone telling you that you are doing good and showing you that you are making progress can make all the difference.

Know what you don't

There is a lot of information out there about music. You could continue to learn forever from the information on the internet alone. Like anything else you haven't learned yet, it is difficult to search for the information that you need. Simply put, you don't know what you don't know. You may end up learning a lot of beneficial things in your search for what you need, but having someone point it out to you, because they already know what you need, can save you so much time. It's interesting that sometimes just the smallest things, like playing a chord in a slightly different way, can make all the difference. Having a teacher show you those little tricks can be a lifesaver.

Push You

This is probably the main reason people get music teachers in the end. We often want to learn things and do things but lack the self discipline to do it ourselves. A piano or guitar teacher that you need to see every week (and pay every week) is pretty good motivation to keep working on your instrument. It's that motivation that a lot of people lack, and a teacher can make all the difference. Along with continuing to practice, a good teacher will help you reach new goals you wouldn't always work on by yourself. This might be memorizing a song, playing in front of people, or just learning a new key. Having someone let you know you can push a little harder can make your overall progress move along so much faster.

Not for Everyone

Getting a music teacher can be a really helpful step for most people, but they aren't for everyone. Some people need teachers and others don't, but most are somewhere in between. Often people need them to start and get a good foundation and could use a break for a while to practice on their own. After a period of practice on their own, some go back to get more lessons to reach that new level. Take classes for a few months, to learn that new skill, and find a teacher to show you that skill specifically.

Learning to Share
(Not what they taught you in preschool.)

Sharing and teaching is part of the natural cycle of learning. It's normal to show or teach someone the things that you have learned. When you are taking lessons from someone, that is something that you should keep in mind. Observe what they do and how they help you. Think about the things that could be improved on. You might end up teaching someday.

I was teaching piano to a high schooler. He had never played any instrument before. He really enjoyed classical music and was doing well. After about a year, he seemed to plateau, and we were trying to figure out what would help him the most. It was almost summer, and since he had extra time, we decided that he might do well teaching some. I was pretty much full on my schedule, and I knew of two young kids who needed lessons. The results were almost immediate. He did fine teaching, of course, but his piano playing got so much better also.

I have found the same to be true in my life. No matter whether it was a song or a new instrument I was learning, if I could teach someone else how to play it, I would learn it ten times more. There is something about teaching something that locks it in your mind in a different way. It's that extra step of needing to figure out how to explain something that really shows if you know it or not.

It's for this reason that sharing is a part of the Speaking Music Method. It doesn't matter if you are starting for the first time or have learned in the past, sharing what you are learning will help you. This is the entire reason for recitals. My recitals were usually at a local coffee shop, and they felt a lot more like open mics than the traditional recital does. I was always surprised, that after the recital, my students would have a sudden surge forward. This was both from the excitement of performing but also from seeing others do it and being inspired by that. Creativity creates more creativity. Sharing a little bit of what you have learned will spark more things for you to learn.

Exercise #1
What do you want to learn

Think about what you want to learn from your teacher exactly. You won't learn forever from them, and going into lessons with specific goals will get you the most out of your time with the teacher.

This goes back to your goals section. I wouldn't try to learn something specific from a teacher that will take more than a year. So think about your overall goal and break it down, if necessary, to what you would like to accomplish in about a half of a year. Whether your goal is a piece of your larger goal or just something small, let them know what you are looking for.

This is going to get you on track so much faster and make your experience with them better.

Exercise #2
Do you need a Teacher?

(Audiobook Friendly) Decide if you need an instructor. What ways will they help and what are the pros and cons to using an instructor in your personal situation?

This is going to combine several things we have already done. Think about both your goals and your learning style. Are you someone who will need extra encouragement, affirmations, structure, or knowledge from a teacher? Are you someone who will enjoy figuring things out yourself?

This will change your first steps in learning music, but doesn't need to be permanent. You can always take lessons for a while and then learn on your own for a while. Don't feel that you need to choose one path forever.

Exercise #3
What did you Learn?

(Introvert Friendly) Condense what you have learned so far about learning music on a single paper.

Being able to condense and simplify what you have learned, like you are teaching someone else, will solidify it in your mind. There is nothing like teaching someone else something to show yourself how much you know it.

In this exercise you can either write down what you have learned or you can actually teach someone else it.

Recap

Music teachers don't know everything about music. They also don't know everything about you and what you need. Like many things in life, it is up to you to decide what to learn and how to learn it. This all starts with your goals and learning style. Once you decide what your goals are, you can start finding the right type of teacher to get you there.

No matter if you think of yourself as self taught or not, your learning is in your own hands. If you only learn what your teacher tells you to, then if you stop your lessons for a period of time, you will stop learning. Learning how to practice and learn on your own is often the difference between a person who learns music and one who "took lessons once."

Affirmation Statement

Belief:

What you believe will shape how you learn and how far you will go. Believing that you can learn music is more important than your talent, connections, or background.

If you have a desire to learn music, that is proof in itself that you have the ability to learn it.

If you maintain your belief that you can learn music as you work towards your goals, you will continually be making progress towards them.

Goals:

There are infinite things you can learn in music, and your personal goals will allow you to learn what is relevant to you. They will help you make progress towards what is meaningful to you personally. Goals that are based on emotional health and desire will make it more likely that you will continue learning and allow for your music to become a part of your life instead of a chore.

Learn:

The majority of material that you learn will be based on the goals you have set and will continually bring you closer to those goals.

Breaking up what you learn into separate sections will make you learn each quality better.

Music theory for knowledge

Sheet Music for communication

Muscle Memory for consistency

Rhythm for function

Ear Training for Optionality

And Creativity for self-expression

The style and method that you learn your instrument with should be based on how you personally learn best. Many of the things you will learn don't need to be learned while touching your instrument and can be taken with you anywhere.

Each new thing you learn allows you the opportunity to learn countless more things.

We have learned so many things in our lives already, and music is no different. Take that as assurance that you can learn what you want to in music, just as you have learned so many things in the past.

Practice:

Muscle memory combines what we have learned with a simple practice, making it so that we don't have to think about each individual part of music. We can let our muscles do a lot of the work.

How you practice will be the defining difference between succeeding in learning music and not. It is something that every musician has needed to do.

Practice is something that can and should be fun and enjoyable to do. For most musicians, practice will be how they play the majority of their music.

Basic consistent practice, combined with the belief that you can learn music, will allow you to reach any goal you set.

Share:

The final step to learning something is being able to share what you have learned with someone else. If you can explain what you have learned to someone else, then you will understand it so much better.

Share what you are learning with others, even if that is just posting online what song you are learning at the moment.

Chapter #9: Conclusion

"Music is the universal language of
mankind"
Henry Wadsworth Longfellow

There you go. Now all you have to do is learn the universal language of mankind. That shouldn't be a problem at all, because it will be fun.

I have worked with a lot of musicians and have played on a lot of stages in my life. I haven't found a rhyme or reason to when you get really hurtful comments and "constructive criticism." It isn't usually the drunk yelling about how you suck that means much to me. It usually comes from the artist I respect saying that it isn't worth it for me to try, because no one can make a good living in music anymore. Or it's the sibling who says, at some point,

I should face reality because, I should know, that our family isn't talented enough to make it big. You will run into these moments when you start to work towards your dreams. The best advice I have for you, when you run into that, is "Don't feed the trolls."

 Everything takes a certain amount of time. Don't get discouraged or doubt yourself just because it is taking longer than you think it should take.

Remember that you can learn the instrument you want and reach the goals you are setting for yourself. Everything that you will be learning is available for you, and all you have to do is believe and work towards it. You aren't going to reach the end when you start, but if you start working towards it, there is no telling how far you will go. Once again, there has never been a student that I have worked with that couldn't learn music.

"Music is the shorthand of emotion."
Leo Tolstoy

As a recap, it all starts with our belief. If we don't believe we can do it, then there is little chance we will. You can learn music, and it is this thought and belief that you will feel when you work on each part of your music. When you do research to see what music teachers are in your area, you can do it with the faith that this is one of the steps on your journey to playing music. You are joining the countless people in the past that have been making music for thousands of years.

There are infinite things that you can learn about music. Trying to learn it all is not typically the most efficient way to go about it. It comes down to what you want to learn and what your goals are. Take time now to think about what you want to play. Try to picture where you would play and who you would play with. All of these things will affect what you will start to learn and how you will progress. You should be able to picture your goals and work towards the emotions and lifestyle of the person you will be when you accomplish them. It is the goals you make and the belief that you can accomplish them that will continue to move you forward.

Once you know what your goals are, your learning begins. There are some basics of sheet music and music theory that you can learn anytime and anywhere. These will help you progress with your instrument, but the practice you do everyday is what will make the biggest difference.

You can break up your practice into different sections so you can learn each part better. Try to work on things that can give you muscle memory. This will allow your body to help you as your mind is learning new and exciting things. You can learn rhythm and music theory by muscle memory exercises and continually be enjoying making music from day one.

You can learn to be creative in your exercises and learn ways to improvise with your exercises. As you work on these beginning steps, you will learn more things that you can learn. It's this snowball effect that will make it so you will never run out of things to learn.

You can see that there isn't any reason you can't learn the instrument you want or any instrument after that. You just need to follow these basic steps, with the belief that you can do it, and work towards your goal, knowing that you will reach it.

One final time, let's look at our statement in closing.

Affirmation Statement

Belief:

What you believe will shape how you learn and how far you will go. Believing that you can learn music is more important than your talent, connections, or background.

If you have a desire to learn music, that is proof in itself that you have the ability to learn it.

If you maintain your belief that you can learn music as you work towards your goals, you will continually be making progress towards them.

Goals:

There are infinite things you can learn in music, and your personal goals will allow you to learn what is relevant to you. They will help you make progress towards what is meaningful to you personally. Goals that are based on emotional health and desire will make it more likely that you will continue learning and allow for your music to become a part of your life instead of a chore.

Learn:

The majority of material that you learn will be based on the goals you have set and will continually bring you closer to those goals. Breaking up what you learn into separate sections will make you learn each quality better.

Music theory for knowledge
Sheet Music for communication
Muscle Memory for consistency
Rhythm for function
Ear Training for Optionality
And Creativity for self-expression

The style and method that you learn your instrument with should be based on how you personally learn best. Many of the things you will learn don't need to be learned while touching your instrument and can be taken with you anywhere.

Each new thing you learn allows you the opportunity to learn countless more things.

We have learned so many things in our lives already, and music is no different. Take that as assurance that you can learn what you want to in music, just as you have learned so many things in the past.

Practice:

Muscle memory combines what we have learned with a simple practice, making it so that we don't have to think about each individual part of music. We can let our muscles do a lot of the work.

How you practice will be the defining difference between succeeding in learning music and not. It is something that every musician has needed to do.

Practice is something that can and should be fun and enjoyable to do. For most musicians, practice will be how they play the majority of their music.

Basic consistent practice, combined with the belief that you can learn music, will allow you to reach any goal you set.

Share:

 The final step to learning something is being able to share what you have learned with someone else. If you can explain what you have learned to someone else, then you will understand it so much better.

Share what you are learning with others, even if that is just posting online what song you are learning at the moment.

Appendix

    I've been told that too much information all at once can be both overwhelming and not helpful. It's because of this that I couldn't add many of the things that I would want to. I would want to have all the information available to you to learn:

- Your specific instrument and the notes on it
- Finger exercises for that instrument
- Rhythm exercises
- Specific layouts to practices for reaching your specific goals
- How to play each instrument
- Sheet Music
- Music Theory

    Unfortunately, I can't add these things in one experience. It would be too much for most anyone. This book was designed to help you understand what there is to learn about and to diagnose where you personally need to start learning. Now you should know where you want to go in music and what you need to get you there.

    I am going to add a few resources here in the appendix (That's what it's for anyway, right?) It is very likely these resources will be enough to get you started. If you want to go further, you can find more books and classes from me on our website www.speakingmusic.online

For Sheet Music and Music Theory, check out the book "**Music Theory for the Average Musician.**" It contains everything that the average musician will need to know about both sheet music or music theory. You can find it on the website or Amazon.

If you learn better from video and audio, then I suggest the members section of the website. In that area we have video classes for:

- Sheet Music
- Music Theory
- Piano
- Voice
- Guitar
- Ukulele
- Kalimba (Thumb Harp)
- Ocarina
- Recorder

Those classes are great but they are just information. As I hope you've seen through the book so far, it isn't enough to have the information. You need to know what your goals are and go towards that.

Since this is such an important part I want to help you out a little further. I've made a questionnaire that you can fill out and I'll look over it for you. I will send you an analysis of what you should learn based on your answers. Just go to https://www.speakingmusic.online/assessment and you can fill it out there.

Sheet Music

As we have said before, sheet music is the written form of music. We are going to look at just a few things to get you started with sheet music. We will look at the notes in the treble clef, sharps and flats, and the timing of the notes.

Note Names in the Treble Clef

We will look at both the lines and the spaces.

Looking at the treble clef the spaces spell out FACE.
I really like this way of looking at it because you can easily and quickly see each note at a glance

To learn the lines many people use acronyms to remember the lines. Starting at the bottom we have (E) Every (G) Good (B) Boy (D) Deserves (F) Fudge.

Every Good Boy Deserves Fudge
E   G   B   D   F

Every Note in Our Music

The twelve notes we use are;　A, A#(Bb), B, C, C#(Db), D, D#(Eb), E, F, F#(Gb), G, G#(Ab)

These are all the notes that we use in western music. We do repeat these notes higher or lower in different "Octaves" but they are the same notes just higher or lower.

On sheet music, we only have lines and spaces that show "natural" notes. These notes are A, B, C, D, E, F, G. We also use notes with sharps and flats.

Flats bring a note one half-step down, and a sharp brings it one half-step up. The basic way to see this is to have a note and put a sharp or flat next to it.

Flat　　　　　Sharp

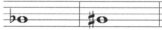

Note Timing

Many songs are in 4/4 timing - as seen below. The top section is the timing of the notes, and the bottom section are rests (when you don't play anything)

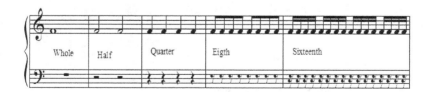

| Whole | Half | Quarter | Eigth | Sixteenth |

Music Theory

There is obviously a lot you can learn in music theory, but we all need to start somewhere. I think, if everyone knew how to make a scale and the chords in that scale it would just be amazingly helpful for every musician. In order to just learn those two things we will need to learn:

- Steps (whole and half)
- Major Scale
- Minor/Major 3rds
- Chords
- Chord order in the Scale

Whole and Half Steps

 With a Half Step (H) you only go from one note to the next. With a Whole step (W) you skip a note.

Major Scale

A Major Scale is made up of seven steps in this order.

W H W W W H W

So the Major C scale would be C D E F G A B C

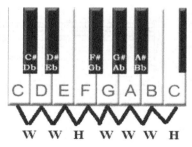

Chords

Basic chords are made up of Major and Minor 3rds.

Major 3rd

A Major third is made up of two whole steps.

A Minor third is made up of a whole step and a half step

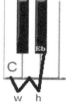

Major Chord

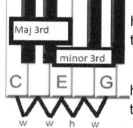

A Major Chord first has a Major 3rd and then a Minor 3rd.

A Minor Chord first has a Minor 3rd and then a Major 3rd

Minor Chord

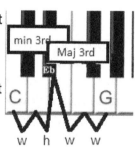

191

Chords in a Scale

The chords are built off the notes in the scale. A Major Scale has 7 notes and so it has 7 chords built off of it. The order of minor and major chords never changes for major scales. It goes:

1 Major, 2 minor, 3 minor, 4 Major, 5 Major, 6 minor, 7 dim

In the C Scale it would be:

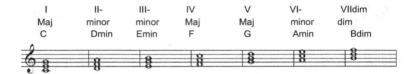

I	II-	III-	IV	V	VI-	VIIdim
Maj	minor	minor	Maj	Maj	minor	dim
C	Dmin	Emin	F	G	Amin	Bdim

There is so much you can do with just this basic knowledge of sheet music and music theory. Not much can be done with it, unless you are learning an instrument and start linking this knowledge with your instrument. This all comes back down to practice.

Once again, if you need more info on learning these things, then check it out on the website. www.speakingmusic.online

Want Micah Blake to be the next
keynote speaker at your next event?

"Unlock the Music Within"

Get connected with him @
speakingmusic.online/speaking

Made in the USA
Middletown, DE
23 August 2024

59039761R00109